D1564398

# CHIEF JOSEPH

## Recent Titles in Greenwood Biographies

# CHIEF JOSEPH

## A Biography

Vanessa Gunther

GREENWOOD BIOGRAPHIES

 GREENWOOD

AN IMPRINT OF ABC-CLIO, LLC
Santa Barbara, California • Denver, Colorado • Oxford, England

**Library of Congress Cataloging-in-Publication Data**

Gunther, Vanessa Ann.
    Chief Joseph : a biography / Vanessa Gunther.
        p. cm. — (Greenwood biographies)
    Includes bibliographical references and index.
    ISBN 978-0-313-37920-8 (hard copy : alk. paper) — ISBN 978-0-313-37921-5 (ebook)   1. Joseph, Nez Perce chief, 1840–1904—Juvenile literature.   2. Nez Perce Indians—Biography—Juvenile literature.   3. Nez Perce Indians—Wars, 1877—Juvenile literature.   I. Title.
    E99.N5J5834   2010
    979.5004'974124'0092—dc22
    [B]        2010015898

ISBN: 978-0-313-37920-8
EISBN: 978-0-313-37921-5

14   13   12   11   10      1   2   3   4   5

This book is also available on the World Wide Web as an eBook.
Visit www.abc-clio.com for details.

Greenwood
An Imprint of ABC-CLIO, LLC

ABC-CLIO, LLC
130 Cremona Drive, P.O. Box 1911
Santa Barbara, California 93116-1911

This book is printed on acid-free paper ∞

Manufactured in the United States of America

*To Michael, Alexander, Selene, Alec, and Sebastian.*
*May you inherit the world that Joseph envisioned.*

# CONTENTS

# SERIES FOREWORD

In response to high school and public library needs, Greenwood developed this distinguished series of full-length biographies specifically for student use. Prepared by field experts and professionals, these engaging biographies are tailored for high school students who need challenging yet accessible biographies. Ideal for secondary school assignments, the length, format, and subject areas are designed to meet educators' requirements and students' interests.

Greenwood offers an extensive selection of biographies spanning all curriculum-related subject areas including social studies, the sciences, literature and the arts, history and politics, as well as popular culture, covering public figures and famous personalities from all time periods and backgrounds, both historic and contemporary, who have made an impact on American and/or world culture. Greenwood biographies were chosen based on comprehensive feedback from librarians and educators. Consideration was given to both curriculum relevance and inherent interest. The result is an intriguing mix of the well known and the unexpected, the saints and sinners from long-ago history and contemporary pop culture. Readers will find a wide array of subject choices from fascinating crime figures like Al Capone to inspiring pioneers like Margaret

Mead, from the greatest minds of our time like Stephen Hawking to the most amazing success stories of our day like J. K. Rowling.

While the emphasis is on fact, not glorification, the books are meant to be fun to read. Each volume provides in-depth information about the subject's life from birth through childhood, the teen years, and adulthood. A thorough account relates family background and education, traces personal and professional influences, and explores struggles, accomplishments, and contributions. A timeline highlights the most significant life events against a historical perspective. Bibliographies supplement the reference value of each volume.

# INTRODUCTION

The history of America would not be complete without a rendition of the exploits of Meriwether Lewis and William Clark. In May 1804, accompanied by three dozen men, they set out across the still undiscovered land that would become part of the western United States in order to create maps and discover what the land held for the fledgling nation. America was still in its infancy when Lewis and Clark came across the Nez Perce Indians in the late summer of 1805. The American Revolution had concluded only a single generation earlier. In that short generation, after the United States had won its independence from Great Britain, it had suffered a depression and engendered serious doubts among European nations about whether this new experiment in republicanism would survive. However, survive it did, and it flourished. With the purchase of the Louisiana Territory from France in 1803, the United States became the third-largest nation on earth at the time. Imbued with a sense of purpose that would later be called *manifest destiny*, Americans set out to occupy the space between the two great oceans, the Atlantic and the Pacific. Before this occupation could begin in earnest, however, Lewis and Clark were dispatched by President Thomas Jefferson to explore the nation's newest acquisition and to chronicle their findings so the generations to follow would be prepared for the long journey ahead. Midway through their journey, a tired and bedraggled Lewis and Clark and the Corps of Discovery stumbled upon, rather than *discovered,* the Nez Perce Indians. Because of the generosity shown by the Nez Perce, Lewis and Clark were able to complete their journey to the Pacific Ocean and return safely to the nation from which they had come. The chance meeting between these two peoples, the Americans and the Nez Perce would change the story of America and introduce the growing nation to one of the most unique and farsighted leaders the land has ever produced, Chief Joseph.

His name was *In-mut-too-yah-lat-lat.* In the language of his people, it means "Thunder rising above lofty mountains," and few men have been more aptly named than he. To the white population in America, however, he was known only as Joseph, chief of the Nez Perce Indians and the architect of one of the most pivotal events in the 19th century, the flight of the Nez Perce Indians in 1877. To most Americans at the time, the Nez Perce story seemed simple enough; when faced with the loss of their tribal lands and confronted by the advance of American civilization, the Indians fled. The image of these *noble savages* trying desperately to cling to the remnants of their dying civilization may have been the way most sympathetic whites would come to view the flight of the Nez Perce; however, their story began decades before that fateful summer in 1877. Unfortunately, most Americans were not interested in learning about the treaties that had divested the Indians of their land; the near impossible requests that had been made by the commander of the military forces in the region, the Civil War general Oliver Otis Howard; or even the cruel treatment they had been forced to endure at the hands of settlers. Unable to reason with General Howard, unwilling to live on a reserve of land, and unable to remain on their traditional lands, many of the Nez Perce people followed Joseph on a 1,500-mile odyssey that took them from their traditional homes in Oregon and Idaho to the windswept prairie of northern Montana in a desperate bid to reach sanctuary in Canada. During their three-and-a-half-month ordeal, the Nez Perce defeated four U.S. armies and created a legend that endures to this day. To Americans unfamiliar with tribal power structures, they could attribute the phenomenal success of the Indians to only one person, Chief Joseph. To white America, Joseph led blistering attacks that soundly defeated the military forces of the nation and then resolutely turned to continue his journey to the north. All of that would change on October 5, 1877. While the image of a "Red Napoleon" had already been established in the minds of most Americans at the time, the surrender of the Nez Perce took on a romantic visage as an unbowed Joseph proudly approached Howard, presented him with his rifle, and proclaimed, "From this day forward, I will fight no more forever." Stirring words and a panoramic scene worthy of the best Hollywood might have to offer, but the flight of the Nez Perce, their defeat of the armies of the United States, and the surrender of Joseph in the face of overwhelming odds did not happen because of or in the way that popular history remembers it.

It is perhaps because of the power of the images that grew around Joseph at the time and since that a legend was created. Like most legends, Joseph seemed almost to defy the limits of humanity. Much of what has been popularly attributed to Chief Joseph comes from newspaper reports that were dispatched from the field during that fateful summer. Later, Joseph would also recognize the power of this medium to spread the message about the plight of his people in the aftermath of their attempted escape to Canada. Forced to live in what the Nez Perce called the *Eeikish Pah* or the "hot place," more than 25 percent of their people died, and it seemed they would never again see the cool meadows and mountains of their homeland. Using the newspapers and playing on American perceptions of the Indians, Joseph was able to successfully negotiate a return to the region, but not to the exact land of their ancestors. Throughout the years of struggle, Joseph and the Nez Perce represent the enduring spirit of humanity when faced with insurmountable odds. While our recollections are marred by ideas of how we wanted or imagined things to be, not as they actually were, the story of Joseph and the Nez Perce is no less compelling. In the case of Chief Joseph and the Nez Perce, the perceptions and misunderstandings we have are the remnants of the ideas we have held for almost a century and a half. This book will attempt to clarify the ambiguities of the flight of the Nez Perce and the leadership of one of their most extraordinary leaders, Chief Joseph.

# TIMELINE: EVENTS IN THE LIFE OF CHIEF JOSEPH

| | |
|---|---|
| **10,000 B.C.** | Nez Perce enter the Columbia River Plateau. |
| **A.D. 1755** | Smallpox epidemic destroys up to 50 percent of the Nez Perce. |
| **1760** | Smallpox epidemic in Columbia Plateau. |
| **1770–1780** | Horses are introduced to the Columbia Plateau Indians. |
| **1781** | Smallpox epidemic in Columbia Plateau. |
| **1785** | Tuekakas (Joseph's father) is born. |
| **1805** | September–October—Lewis and Clark meet the Nez Perce in the Weippe Prairie. |
| **1806** | May—Lewis and Clark return to the Nez Perce camps. |
| **1807** | David Thompson establishes a fur-trading outpost for the North West Company of Montreal. |
| **1815** | Smohalla born into the Wanapum tribe and achieves prominence as a medicine man and spiritual leader. He would become the founder of the Dreamer religion. |
| **1821** | Hudson Bay Company merges with the North West Company of Montreal and extends their presence in the Northwest. |
| | John West establishes the Red River Mission. |

**1825** The first Indian students from the Kutenai and Spokan tribes are admitted to the Red River Mission.

**1830** The first Nez Perce students are sent to the Red River Mission.

**1831** Four Nez Perce delegates journey to St. Louis to request missionaries come to the Columbia Plateau.

**1834** Reverend Jason Lee begins missionary activity in Columbia Plateau.

**1836** Whitman and Spalding missionary activity begins among the Nez Perce.

Catholic priests establish first Catholic church at Champoeg, Oregon.

**1837** Henry Spalding whips Blue Cloak and almost destroys the Spalding Mission.

Catholic missionaries begin ministering among the Nez Perce.

Elijah White arrives to assist Jason Lee's missionary efforts.

**1839** Tuekakas is baptized by Henry Spalding.

Asa B. Smith establishes the Kamiah Mission.

Measles outbreak among the Indians of the Columbia Plateau.

**1840s** Fur trade in Pacific Northwest collapses.

**1840** Chief Joseph is born (March) and baptized by Henry Spalding (April).

Joseph Frost establishes the Clatsop Mission.

**1841** Ollokot (Joseph's brother) is baptized by Henry Spalding.

Elijah White is forced to resign from mission.

**1842** Elijah White returns to Oregon Territory as the Indian subagent for the region and brings 100 new settlers.

**1843** Elijah White attempts to establish Ellis as the chief for all the Nez Perce people.

Marcus Whitman returns from a visit to the East Coast with 1,000 new settlers.

**1844–1846** Some 5,000 settlers enter into the Oregon Territory.

**1846** Kamiah Mission is closed due to limited Indian participation.

1847   Measles outbreak.
       Some 4,000–5,000 settlers enter the Columbia Plateau.
       November—Massacre at the Whitman Mission and be-
       ginning of the Cayuse War (1848–1855).
1848   Chief Joseph (age 8) attends the Lapwai Peace Confer-
       ence with his father.
1850   Oregon Donation Act allows settlers to claim land in Or-
       egon.
       Five Cayuse warriors are executed for their role in the
       Whitman Massacre.
       Tuekakas (Old Joseph) returns his people to the Wal-
       lowa Valley.
1851   Gold is found in Nez Perce territory.
1853   Isaac Stevens is appointed as governor and superinten-
       dent of Indian Affairs of the newly established Wash-
       ington Territory.
1855   Walla Walla Treaty Council—Nez Perce cede 6 million
       acres to the government.
1860   Gold is discovered in the Clearwater area.
1861   U.S. government establishes the Nez Perce Indian
       Agency.
1862–1863   Chief Joseph marries Heyoon yoyikt.
1863   Thief Treaty— Chief Lawyer (Nez Perce) agrees to cede
       more than 8 million acres to the government.
       Chief Joseph participates in the Thief Treaty council
       but refuses to sign the treaty.
       Tuekakas (Old Joseph) rejects Christianity.
1865   Chief Joseph's first child, Hophoponmi, is born.
1868   Chief Lawyer (Nez Perce) secures the Treaty of 1868
       granting the best Nez Perce lands to his band.
1869–1876   Grant's Peace Policy is in effect.
1871   Tuekakas (Old Joseph) dies in August.
       Henry Spalding reopens the Lapwai Mission.
       White settlers move into the Imnaha Valley.
1872   Meeting brokered between white settlers and Chief Jo-
       seph does not succeed in removing settlers from the land
       belonging to Chief Joseph's band.

**1872–1873** Modoc Indian War.

**1873** Gold is found in the land surrounding the Wallowa Valley.

Ulysses S. Grant designates land in the Wallowa Valley for the exclusive use of Chief Joseph's band.

**1874** Oliver Otis Howard enters the Pacific Northwest as the commander of the Department of the Columbia.

**1875** Howard and Chief Joseph meet for the first time on the Umatilla Reservation.

Public outcry forces Grant to rescind the order for the Wallowa Reservation.

U.S. government begins construction of a wagon road through the Wallowa Valley.

**1876** Rancher A. B. Findley and Wells McNall are involved in the murder of Wilhautyah.

June—Battle of Little Big Horn.

Howard demands Nez Perce move onto reservations.

**1877** January—Chief Joseph is ordered to surrender to the reservation by April.

April—Meeting between Chief Joseph and Howard at the Lapwai Mission results in arrest of Toohoolhoolzote and orders for the Indians to present themselves to the reservations by June.

June—Last Grand Council at Split Rocks and the murder of several white men by Wahkitits.

Chief Joseph's wife Toma Alwawonmi gives birth to Joseph's second daughter.

June–October—Flight of the Nez Perce from the Wallowa Valley to Montana to escape pursuing U.S. Army forces.

October 5—Chief Joseph and his band surrender to Howard.

November—Chief Joseph speaks publically about the Nez Perce flight for the first time.

**1877–1878** Nez Perce are moved to Fort Keogh, then Fort Abraham Lincoln, and then to Fort Leavenworth.

1878    Summer—Nez Perce are moved to Baxter Springs, Oklahoma. By the end of the summer, Chapman begins a letter-writing campaign to move Joseph's people to better land.

1879    January—Chief Joseph makes his first journey to Washington, D.C., to demand to return to his people's lands in the Wallowa Valley.

        June—Joseph's people are moved to Oakland Reserve in Indian Territory.

1880    Presbyterian Church becomes involved in the plight of the Nez Perce.

1881    Christianized Nez Perce led by James Reuben begin to assume control over Joseph's people.

        Joseph's baby daughter dies.

1883    Thirty-three Christianized Nez Perce are allowed to return to the Columbia Plateau.

1884    July—Congress authorizes the return of the rest of the Nez Perce to the Columbia Plateau.

1885    May—The remaining Nez Perce begin their journey home. The Christianized Nez Perce will live at the Lapwai Reservation, and the non-Christianized Indians will live on the Colville Reservation in Washington.

1897    Chief Joseph speaks at the dedication of Grant's Tomb.

1900    Chief Joseph is allowed to return to the Wallowa Valley for the first time since 1877.

1903    Chief Joseph performs in Wild Bill Cody's Wild West Show.

1904    September 21—Chief Joseph dies on the Colville Reservation age 64.

# Chapter 1

# THE NEZ PERCE WORLD
# BEFORE CONTACT

## NEZ PERCE ARRIVAL IN THE UNITED STATES AND EARLY LIFE

The Nez Perce Indians have lived in the Columbia River Plateau region of the United States for more than 10,000 years. Many scholars believe that during the last ice age, people crossed the Bering Strait when ice formed an extensive bridge between Asia and the Americas. When the ice began to recede approximately 10,000 years ago, the land bridge was lost and the people who had crossed became the ancestors of the American Indians.

The Nez Perce were one of the groups that migrated from Asia to America. They are classified as part of the Penutian language group, which includes Indians who primarily live in the Pacific Northwest, but also have related linguistic groups as far south as California. For this reason, many researchers believe that the Nez Perce are not one distinct cultural group, but a composite of several groups. By the time Lewis and Clark met the tribe in 1805, they occupied more than 17 million acres of land in what is now Washington, Oregon, Montana, and Idaho. It was Lewis and Clark who first misidentified the tribe by the name Nez Perce.

Nez Perce was the general name given by French fur trappers in the area to the tribes they encountered. While the name Nez Perce is often translated as "pierced nose" there is little to suggest that this was a wide spread cultural practice of these Indians. Instead, it was a cultural trait of the Chinook tribe, which also lived along the Columbia River and occupied the territory north of the Nez Perce. Today most Nez Perce people call themselves *Nim-ipuu*, which means simply "real people." However, this is not the name by which the Nez Perce originally knew themselves. Prior to the introduction of horses in the 18th century, the tribe called itself *Cuupn-itpel-uu*, or "walked out of the mountains."

In the years before the white man came, the Nez Perce people traveled seasonally from the deep river gorges of the Snake, Clearwater, and Salmon rivers into the protected valleys of Idaho and Washington. There, according to the Nez Perce warrior *Wottolen* or "Hair Combed over Eyes," they lived primarily along two waterways, the *Kakayohneme* Creek, which is at the head of the Clearwater River, and around *Tannish* near the Salmon River. When Lewis and Clark encountered the tribe, they estimated their numbers to be 4,000. However, scholars have placed the tribe's membership at closer to 6,000. This would have made the Nez Perce one of the most powerful tribal groups in the region.

## DIVISION OF THE TRIBE

As the tribe grew, it divided into those who lived in the upper Clearwater River basin and those who lived in the Wallowa Valley in modern Oregon. Within these two general groups, smaller bands formed and were generally identified by the river or tributary that they lived near. Each of these bands was autonomous, or self-governing, and lived in villages where their populations ranged from 50 to 200 individuals. Most of the members of these village bands descended from related family groups.

At the time Lewis and Clark arrived, approximately 40–70 villages existed in the region. However, archaeological excavation has revealed more than 300 village sites that can be attributed to the Nez Perce over the centuries. Carbon dating has identified human residence along the Snake River as long as 11,000 years ago, and many researchers suggest human habitation in the region could be longer. On the canyon walls that form the boundaries of the Snake River, more than a hundred pictographs remain as silent testimony to the longevity of human habitation in the region. While the meaning of the pictographs has been lost to time, the descendants of the people who drew them have continued to live in the region for more than 500 generations.

## THE HEART OF A MONSTER: THE NEZ PERCE CREATION STORY

Despite the conclusions of archaeologists and scientists, for the Nez Perce themselves their entrance into the Columbia Plateau had little to do with frozen land bridges between continents, or the evidence presented through carbon dating. In the words of Yellow Wolf, one of the warriors who belonged to Joseph's band, "We came from no country, as have the whites. We were always here."[1]

In the traditional creation story of the tribe, in an era before modern time began, the world was much different than today. The great spirit of the Nez Perce, *Hanyawat,* created the world, but within it he placed animals and inanimate objects, all of which were capable of communication and interaction. In this world, modern humans had yet to appear, but their potential seems to have always been waiting in the shadows.

The place where the Nez Perce came into being is a mound along the Kamiah Creek, an area that the Nez Perce call simply the "heart." This mound was once the heart of a monster that was so vast it encompassed all the land in the surrounding valley. So large and powerful was the monster that it did not need to leave the creek or move about to hunt for food. It simply inhaled and drew to it animals from miles away. The monster consumed so many animals that it seemed to the early inhabitants of the earth that the monster would soon consume all the earth.

One day Coyote, or *'Itseyéeye,* was building a fish ladder for the salmon to use to travel up stream when a voice called out to him to stop, it said that the monster had eaten everyone and there was no longer any point to his labors. Coyote ceased his labors and at that moment resolved to defeat the monster and to retrieve those whom the monster had eaten. Coyote devised a plan that would call for him to be eaten by the monster as well. To make himself more appealing and tasty to the monster, he took a bath. Once clean he began to make his way to Kamiah Creek.

When he had reached Kamiah Creek, Coyote remained hidden in the grass and there gazed upon the monster for the first time.

Never in his life had Coyote seen anything so large. To avoid detection by the enormous creature, Coyote concealed himself in the ridges and mountains that surrounded the creek until he had surveyed the monster from all angles. Satisfied that he now knew how to defeat the monster, Coyote took some rawhide rope and tied one end around himself and the other ends around three mountains, Pilot Knob, Seven Devil's Mountain, and Cottonwood Butte. Then Coyote filled a pack with five knives and a flint for making fire. When he had finished his preparations, Coyote called out to the monster and invited the beast to inhale him as well. However, Coyote made his offer while still concealed in the grass, and the monster could not see him. Suspecting a trap and wanting to determine who his brash new adversary was, the monster offered instead to have coyote inhale him.

Undaunted by the task, Coyote tried, several times, but failed to even move the great beast. Once Coyote gave up his attempts, the monster smugly began to inhale, and his breath soon carried Coyote from his place in the grasses and toward what seemed certain death.

However, all of this was part of Coyote's plan. Instead of panicking and struggling against the breath of the monster as he was drawn through the air and toward the monster, Coyote spread camas bulbs and serviceberries in the fields around him. Coyote knew the monster would be defeated and that the time for human beings to come upon the earth had arrived, and they would need something to eat. When Coyote was sucked into the mouth of the monster, one of his ropes became tangled in the monster's teeth. He was in danger of being eaten, but he quickly cut himself free and landed safely in the mouth of the monster, well past his teeth. Once inside, Coyote began to walk down the throat of the beast. As he walked, he noticed a large number of bones scattered about, and he came to understand just how many had died in the belly of the creature.

Coyote soon came upon some boys, and he told them to take him to the heart of the monster. As the boys began to lead him, grizzly bear rushed out toward him and tried to frighten him. Coyote, however, was not frightened; instead, he was disappointed in the bullying behavior of the bear and its unwillingness to fight the beast. Coyote kicked the bear on the nose and flattened it, and the bear went away. Then a rattlesnake shook its rattle at Coyote. Undaunted, he stomped on its head, flattening it as well; beaten, the snake slithered away. Finally, a brown bear met Coyote on his way to the monster's heart and contemptuously insisted that Coyote would not be able to save the people. Coyote ignored him and continued on his path.

As Coyote traveled, he met several people who spoke to him. Even his old friend the fox appeared and expressed his sadness that his friend had had the misfortune of being eaten like everyone else. When Coyote informed them he would kill the beast, many offered their help. Coyote instructed them to gather anything that would burn, which they did, and soon he had enough to build a fire. By now he had reached the heart of the monster, and there he built a fire and then began to cut away the fat around its heart, which he gave to the people to eat. Soon the smoke from the fire began to fill the beast and stung its eyes and filled its nose. The monster knew that Coyote was to blame for his discomfort, and the monster tried to cast him out, but Coyote would not go. As the fire built in intensity, the monster began to feel more and more uncomfortable and begged Coyote to leave his body. However, Coyote refused and continued to cut away at the monster's heart because he knew that if he stopped the beast would recover and take out his anger on the people.

Despite Coyote's preparations, the heart of the monster proved to be so strong that in succession each of his knives broke, until he was left with only one. Furiously, Coyote continued his task before his last knife broke. He could feel the power of the monster beginning to wane and knew it was time to prepare the people to enter the world. As he worked, Coyote instructed the people to gather up all the bones of those who had died and be prepared to take those with them when the monster died. The people did as they were told and then gathered to wait. When Coyote had almost finished his task of cutting up the monster's heart, his last knife broke, but instead of giving up, he seized the last remnant of the monster's heart and destroyed it with his bare hands. With a pitiful groan, the monster exhaled sharply, expelling all the people inside, and then died.

Once outside the monster, Coyote restored to life those who had died. He then carved up the monster and gave a piece to each group of people around him, and he sent these people out into the country to start

new lives. The remnant of the monster that these people carried with
them would imbue them with skills that would help them to survive in
the land where they would settle. These individuals became the Cayuse, Flathead, Blackfeet, and other Indians of the region.

However, after he had distributed all the parts of the monster, Coyote
still had one group of people left and nothing more to give them. For
those people, Coyote reserved a special gift; he washed the land in water
and then gave it to them and promised that while they may be small in
number, they would always be a powerful people. To the Nez Perce, this
was how the people came to their lands. The individuals who received
the blessing of the water from Coyote became the ancestors of the Nez
Perce, and this is why the Nez Perce consider themselves to be the children of Coyote.

## NEZ PERCE POLITICAL
## AND MILITARY LIFE

As the Nez Perce grew in number, they formed into distinct villages.
Each village was governed by a headman, or chief, who ensured the general welfare of his people. The position of headman or chief was usually
a hereditary position within the band, but this was not always so. If an
individual appeared with stronger leadership talents than the son of the
previous headman, or if the chief died without a son, the position would
transition to a new leader. The character trait most valued in a leader
was that of oratory or persuasion. The chief would be responsible for as-
suring the well-being of the whole tribal group, and obtaining a consensus on any matter would require an individual who had well-developed
skills in this area.

While these political chiefs led their people most of the time, during
time of war, they relinquished power to a war chief who would then
direct the military maneuvers of the tribe. Joseph was a political chief,
not a military chief as many believe.

## NEZ PERCE GENDERED
## AND HIERARCHICAL ROLES

Many also assume that the Nez Perce and other Indians lived an almost
purely egalitarian existence with all people enjoying absolute equality

within the tribe. This too is an incorrect assumption, and often it has prevailed because the Nez Perce did not have the societal means for coercion that were prevalent in American society, such as police or jails. While the tribe had laws and customs, enforcement of these beliefs was dependent on tribal council meetings where tribal members attempted to reach a consensus on the issue before them. The opinion of the people who comprised the band would be considered at these meetings; however, there were also council meetings that occurred where only with the chiefs and elders of the tribe met. It was during these meetings that a new leader might be chosen, or a decision made to engage in war. The hierarchy that existed within Nez Perce society was less apparent than in American society because of the limited and far-flung members of the tribe. However, a social and gendered hierarchy existed.

## Women's Roles in Nez Perce Society

While the position of headman was held by men, women were not without influence in the tribe, and some researchers suggest that women could have been political leaders as well. Women provided much of the food consumed by the tribal group and ensured the maintenance of the home. In their contribution to the well-being of the tribe and the sustenance of their families, women were considered equally as important as men. They had the right to hold property and could choose to marry or divorce if it suited their needs. However, within the tribe, marriage was viewed as a decision to join not only two people together, but also to join two families together. While negotiations for marriages were conducted by the headmen or the families involved, older women within the family would also judge whether the bride would be a compatible match for her husband's family. Because of the involvement of the whole family in choosing a mate and their support of the couple once they had committed to each other, divorces and separations were unusual in Nez Perce society.

## Death Rituals

In Nez Perce society, women were also central to the death rituals of the tribe. Once an individual died, the female members of the deceased would begin to wail. This would signal the beginning of the mourning period, and as other friends and family members learned of the death, they would add their voices to the growing chorus. The body of the deceased was then cleansed and dressed, and the face was painted red; usually, these activities were carried out by female family members. Following the burial of the deceased, a speech would be given by the shaman or the chief that extolled the virtues and accomplishments of the individual. Then the mourners would adjourn for a feast, which had been prepared by the women. During the feast, the home of the deceased would be moved in order to ensure that the spirit of the dead would not have a place to return to, and then their possessions would be given away so that their spirit would not have any ties to the earth. The Nez Perce believed that spirits who did not move on could become malevolent. Many women also held leadership positions within the tribe if they were shamans or religious leaders.

### Influence over Council Decisions

Older women, like older men, were also afforded great respect within the tribe for their experience and sage advice. Lewis and Clark owed their kind treatment at the hands of the Nez Perce to one woman named *Wat-kue-is*, or "She Who Had Returned from a Far Country." Years before, Wat-kue-is had been kidnapped from the Nez Perce and had lived with several Plains Indian tribes before she was able to escape. As she made her way back to her tribe, she encountered a group of white settlers she called the *Soyapo*, or "Covered Ones," because of the hats they wore. These Soyapo treated her kindly and helped her to return to her people. Wat-kue-is's treatment at the hands of the white settlers changed the opinion of the tribal members who argued that the men of the Corps of Discovery should be killed. Instead, the Nez Perce befriended the men and assisted them in the fulfillment of their mission both on their way to the Pacific Ocean and on their return in 1806.

## UNITY AMONG THE BANDS

The decision made by this band of Nez Perce characterized how each individual band related to the world and the other people around them. At the time the Nez Perce first had contact with members of the Corps of Discovery, more than 300 individual villages were in existence. Each village operated as an autonomous unit; however, these village groups also belonged to a confederation that was heavily influenced by the chief who presided over the largest of the villages. Responsibility for the protection and governance of the tribe as a whole was shared by a war chief and a tribal council that was made up of prominent warriors and the headmen from the related villages. When issues appeared that impacted the tribal group, such as war or trade relations, the tribal council attempted to identify a solution to the problem through consensus. The seriousness with which these councils deliberated added weight to their final decisions, and most Nez Perce strove to explicitly follow the resolutions upon which their tribe had agreed.

## Nez Perce Enemies in War and Peace

While the Nez Perce people are very accepting of the customs of other people, they are reticent to impose their beliefs on others or to have beliefs thrust upon them. For this reason, conflict between the Nez Perce Indians and their neighbors in the rugged mountains and valleys of the Columbia Plateau were limited. The wars that did occur most often involved the Shoshone, Bannock, or Paiute Indians who all lived to the south of the Nez Perce. The Shoshone were most often the target of Nez Perce hostility, and this earned the Shoshone the name *Teewalka*, or "an enemy to be fought." Most often, however, these tribes traded instead of waged war. The Shoshone Indians were the first to trade horses with the Nez Perce. However, if a dispute could not be resolved diplomatically, the Nez Perce were also known as fierce and intelligent warriors.

## THE SEARCH FOR FOOD

Survival depended on an astute ability to utilize the vast resources of the land around them, and the Nez Perce were well adapted to their land. They seasonally migrated through the regions in order to gather camas roots, kouse root, and berries from the sides of rivers and meadows. The kouse root was particularly welcomed by the Nez Perce for its parsnip-like taste and because it was often the first fresh food they were

able to enjoy after a long winter of dried food. While individual ownership of land in the same tradition as American land ownership was not
practiced by the Nez Perce, land was not merely left for the taking. The
various bands of the tribe could share in the bounty of the land, but certain areas were reserved for single family use if that area had special
meaning to the family.

## Hunting to Survive

As hunters, the Nez Perce sought out big game because a single animal
would be able to feed more members of their tribe. Often, hunters would
cover themselves in the hides of animals and creep along the ground in
an attempt to get closer to their prey. Despite the patience involved in
this technique, it was not always successful, and a hunter needed to be
ready to take advantage of every opportunity that presented itself. Because of this, the Nez Perce were known for the quality of their bows,
which were said to be strong enough to send an arrow through the body
of a deer. The bows made by the Nez Perce were about three feet long and
made from the curled horn of a mountain goat. The horn was patiently
straightened by steaming it and then wrapping it in sinew to give it
added strength. The arrows used by the Nez Perce were often tipped in the
venom of a rattlesnake, although the venom, when dry, loses it potency.
They hunted for deer, mountain goats, and bears in the meadows and
mountains of their land. Those few individuals who were brave or lucky
enough to kill a grizzly bear were revered by their people and allowed to
wear a necklace of bear claws as a reminder of their prowess.

## The Great Buffalo Hunts

At times hunters left the protected valleys of their homelands and traveled as far as the Great Plains to hunt buffalo. Because of the inherent
danger in hunting the buffalo, the Nez Perce often joined with their traditional allies the Cayuse or the Flathead to pursue the buffalo. At times
the number of warriors on these hunts could number as high as 1,000.
In some instances, men could be gone for years while they pursued the
buffalo along the plains. The trip to the plains was arduous and forced
the Indians to cross the Bitterroot Mountains; however, the Nez Perce
were familiar with the route, and the path created by their frequent

crossing became the basis for the Lolo trail, a route that would eventually lead Lewis and Clark and other settlers into their territory. In addition to hunting with a bow, the Nez Perce were also adept at setting
snares to entrap the smaller game animals in their lands.

## Fishing

Despite the romance that is often associated with Indian hunting, this
was not the primary source of food for the tribe. Only about 10 percent
of the overall food consumed by the Indians came from hunting. Their
primary source of food was gathering the bounty of the land and fishing.
While secondary in importance to the salmon runs, buffalo hunting was
important to the survival of the tribe because it provided meat to sustain
them in the long winter months, covering for their lodges, and fur to trade
with other tribes and later the Europeans who entered the region. This
trade enabled the tribe to obtain weapons and later horses with which
they increased their power and influence in the region.

While hunting was pursued on a continual basis, when the salmon
began their migrations through the rivers in the Columbia Plateau, the
Nez Perce devoted most of their time to harvesting and preserving as
many as they could. The Nez Perce were accomplished fishermen and
used a variety of methods to catch the salmon they needed for survival.
Fishing hooks, weirs, spears, and nets were all used by both men and
women to harvest this abundant food.

## Gathering the Earth's Bounty

The migratory patterns that characterized Nez Perce life were not ran-
dom wanderings. The Nez Perce had a very sophisticated understanding
of the world around them and traveled seasonally in order to collect the
various plants and animal life that would sustain them. Within Nez Perce
society, children as young as three would begin to assist in the gathering
of food for the tribe. This allowed them to learn which plants were to
be harvested and which were to be avoided. This was important since
about 50 percent of the food consumed by the Indians had been gathered in this manner. Because of the importance of gathering food, the
subsistence patterns they practiced were tailored to ensure access to
these harvests.

## Importance of Others in the Quest for Survival

The ability of the Nez Perce to adapt to their traditional lands was important for survival, but it also served as a cultural linchpin for the tribe. The Nez Perce calendar noted when it was time to harvest the tule reeds (March) or when the Chinook salmon would flood into the Columbia River (May). The importance of particular areas in their territory in maintaining their subsistence patterns also served as gathering places for the bands, which would often go months without seeing each other, and thus became central to their religious and cultural ceremonies.

These gatherings were also ways for the Nez Perce to form alliances with other local tribes. These alliances would serve the Nez Perce in time of war and would also serve as a conduit through which new tribal members would travel. Marriages were often arranged during these gatherings, and this helped to solidify friendly relations between the two peoples. So important were these gatherings that many of the prominent members of the tribe came from tribal groups outside Nez Perce bands. Chief Joseph's mother, *Khap-kha-pon-imi*, or "Loose Bark on Trees," was one of these individuals, as she came from the Umatilla tribe, and his grandfather was a member of the Cayuse tribe.

## NEZ PERCE HOUSES AND STYLE

During the winter, the Nez Perce lived in semisubterranean longhouses that were covered in tule reed mats. These longhouses could extend for as much as 150 feet and were divided into several compartments to allow for privacy among the several families who lived within them. By the 18th century, many bands had begun to adapt these longhouses into smaller conical-shaped houses. When not in their winter encampment, the Nez Perce lived in portable lodges that were lighter and could be broken down and transported more easily. Dress for the Nez Perce adapted the resources that were available to them, but indicated a sense of style that was unique to the tribal group. According to William Clark when he met the Nez Perce in 1805, the

> Indians are Stout likely men, handsom women, and verry dressey
> in their way, the dress of the men are a white Buffalow robe or Elk
> Skin dressed with Beeds which are generally white, Sea Shells—i e

Mother of Pirl hung to ther hair and on a pice of otter Skin about their necks hair cerved in two parsels hanging forward over their Sholders, feathers, and different Coloured Paints which they find in their Countrey Generally white Green and light Blue. Some fiew were a Shirt of Dressed Skins and long legins, and Mockersons Painted, which appears to be their winter dress, with a plat of twisted grass about their necks.[2]

Notwithstanding Clark's poor spelling, his impression of the Nez Perce was very favorable.

## NEZ PERCE LAWS AND CUSTOMS

Many Americans in the 19th century held the persistent belief that because Indians lived a transitory life and did not have permanent dwellings they also had no law, religion, or cultural traditions. This misconception was largely the result of cultural prejudice and misunderstanding and has only recently begun to change. However, the Nez Perce had many laws and customs that were similar to those of the Americans they met. According to Chief Joseph, the laws of the Nez Perce "told us to treat all men as they treated us, that we should never be the first to break a bargain, that we should only speak the truth, that is was a shame for one man to take from another his wife or his property without paying for it."[3]

### Cultural Continuity through Song and Story

Much of the tribe's laws and cultural traditions were passed along to the next generation in the form of stories, songs, and dances. These traditions, or *titwatitnáawit*, reinforced Nez Perce ideas about where they came from and what activities that were considered acceptable within their society. For the Nez Perce, most of the spring and summer was spent gathering enough food to enable them to comfortably live through the winter. By the fall, the village groups had begun their return into the protected mountains of the region. There they could harvest fall crops and finish their preparation for the winter ahead.

During the winter months, the village elders educated and entertained the young with stories about the creation of the world or that exemplified the cultural traditions of their people, such as the story of Cottontail Boy and Thunder, in which the idea of marriage is introduced. Many of the stories of the Nez Perce involved animal characters who acted and spoke like human beings. In addition to this anthropomorphic view of animals, the stories of the Nez Perce also gave animation to in-animate features such as the mountains, rivers, and sky. These stories told of the world that existed before the Nez Perce became a people. For the Nez Perce, once the people had been given possession of the earth, the animals became mute, and the landscape ceased to be animated.

However, while the world no longer spoke out loud, the stories of their previous actions were passed along and became the laws and traditions of the Nez Perce people. Among the winter ceremonies that the Nez Perce participated in was the Winter Dance. During this ceremony, individuals would sing the songs they had been taught by their spirit guides. The stories of the Nez Perce also communicated the traditions of the Indian people. Nez Perce people were also not without a means to enforce their cultural norms.

## Punishment

In the Nez Perce community, it was not considered right that parents should strike their children to correct bad behavior. As such, an individ-ual was designated as a *whip man* to mete out corporal punishment when needed. This position was one of honor within the tribe because the in-dividual had to compassionately but realistically determine how much punishment a child deserved. Whip men never struck grown men, as to do so would be to demean them by treating them like children. When American settlers came to the land of the Nez Perce, this is one cultural taboo they frequently violated in an effort to assert their dominance. To the Nez Perce the American practice of whipping as a corporal punish-ment was tantamount to treating them as though they were children.

## RELIGION

The religion of the Nez Perce was difficult for early American settlers to understand. In part, this was because they refused to consider the Indians' religious traditions from the context of their own religious be-liefs. The traditional religious practice of the Nez Perce was called the

*Washani* religion. Central to the Washani religion was a Creator; this Creator was called *Ah-cum-kin-i-ma-me-hut* by the Nez Perce. The Creator of all "sees and hears everything. He never forgets and that hereafter He will give every man a spirit-home. If he has been a good man, he will have a good home; if a bad man, he will have a bad home."[4] The Washani religion centrally held the same beliefs as the religion of the white man, Christianity. This similarity helped missionaries in their efforts to convert the Indians to Christianity. While many elements of the Washani religion were corrupted over time, the religious movement increased in clarity because of the influence of a shaman named *Smohalla*, or "Dreamer," who came from the Wanapum tribe and was influential during the middle of the 19th century.

## Smohalla and the Dreamer Religion

Smohalla was distressed over the negative impact that white culture was having on the Indians of the region. In the Columbia Plateau, traditional and progressive Indians were beginning to divide the once united tribes of his forefathers. He felt that these divisions would eventually lead to the destruction of the Indians as a distinct cultural group. Smohalla left his tribe to meditate and determine what might bring the people back together again. It was on this quest that Smohalla had his first revelation where he was carried into heaven, met with the Creator, and was given a simple message to deliver to the people. The Indians must reject white ways and return to their traditional cultural, religious, and economic practices, or they would all be destroyed. As the years passed, Smohalla grew in his spiritual strength, and his message was highly regarded and followed by traditionalist Indians in the region, including Chief Joseph. One of the characteristics of those who followed Smohalla, or the Dreamer religion, was a distinctive hairstyle in which the hair is combed above the forehead and the rest is allowed to hang in braids or loose. In all the pictures of Joseph that survive, he is sporting this same Dreamer hairstyle.

## The Wayakin or Special Guides

To the adherents of the Dreamer religion, the power of the animals and of the earth itself, while no longer as obvious as during the day of Coyote, had not disappeared and communication with the people on the earth had not ceased. The Nez Perce believed that these powerful entities could still communicate through dreams and visions; however, to hear these voices, an individual needed to prepare through meditation and fasting. In addition to the wisdom of the world around them, the Nez Perce believed each person had a special guide, a *wayakin*. This guide would reveal the special power present in each person.

Understanding what special gifts an individual had were important to the well-being of the tribe because the Nez Perce believed that it was the responsibility of individuals to use their talents for the betterment of their tribe and the world around them. These spirit guides would assist people throughout their lives whenever they were confronted with difficult decisions or were faced with a seemingly overwhelming task, such as war or a council dispute. To summon an individual's wayakin required a spiritual cleansing, and Nez Perce children were prepared for this moment for years through the stories and songs of their people.

To send an unprepared child out to seek answers from the spirit world could lead to disaster, either for the child or the family. When Nez Perce children reached adolescence, they set out on their vision quest. Both boys and girls would take a cold-water bath to prepare themselves mentally and physically for the challenges they would face. From there the initiate would leave the village and travel into the least traveled areas of the Nez Perce territory. Most often those searching for their spirit guides would head toward the mountains surrounding the Kamiah Creek, the Pilot Knob, Cottonwood Butte, and Seven Devil's Mountain, because this was where the Nez Perce came into being as a people.

While on his journey, the seeker might go three or four weeks with little or no food in order to be sufficiently ready to summon his wayakin. Instead of hunting or subsistence activities, an individual was to spend her day in meditation. Despite the inherent dangers of the land, it was believed that the land itself would protect those who sought their spirit guides. The importance of a wayakin is difficult to understand in American culture. As a spiritual entity, the wayakin would help an individual throughout his or her life by revealing undiscovered truths or insights into particular problems. The wayakins of the Nez Perce could be any of the birds and animals or natural features that comprise the forests and meadows of the Nez Perce lands. Those who were successful in finding their wayakin were changed by the experience and often assumed new names to reflect their changed status.

Many individuals attempted vision quests several times before successfully finding their guides, and not all individuals were successful in finding their wayakin. Because of the special nature of the relationship between an individual and his spirit guide, it was rarely discussed with other people out of a concern that this might lessen the power of the wayakin. It was also forbidden for an individual to pretend to have a wayakin when they did not possess one. For the Nez Perce, such a lie could have dire consequences for the individual and the tribe as a whole as this would anger the spirit world. When an individual returned from his spirit quest, he was assisted in a greater understanding of his wayakin by the shaman of the tribe but made no announcement about what he had experienced. The only time an individual might hint at what their wayakin was came during the annual winter spirit dance when a dancer referred to their spirit guide as they entered the dance.

## Shamans

Among the leaders of the Nez Perce Indians were the shamans. Often the advice of a shaman would be sought when a band was facing a difficult decision or had become ill. However, the primary function of the shaman was to assist people in spiritual matters, either those who had been cursed by the evil thoughts of another or who sought to fully understand the power of their wayakin. Both men and women were shamans and achieved their vaulted position within society by repeatedly demonstrating their superior talent for communication with the spirit world.

During the winter dances and ceremonies, those who aspired to be shamans challenged the wayakins of others to determine who had the greater power. When assisting those who had been threatened or sickened by the malevolent powers of others, shamans would summon their wayakin to combat the evil presence. While shamans often assisted people who had fallen ill, they were not traditional healers who used herbs and sweat baths to cure people from sickness. In Nez Perce society, traditional medicine would be turned to first before employing the services of a shaman. Within their culture, the Nez Perce viewed issues of spirituality and power very seriously.

## Cleansing Rituals

For the Nez Perce, the issue of spiritual and physical cleanliness was paramount in their daily as well as spiritual lives. It was only by being cleansed that individuals could successfully engage in the rituals and activities of their daily lives. Bathing in extremely hot water or enduring the scathing temperatures of the sweat lodge were other means through which the Nez Perce prepared themselves for the rigors of the activities they faced. Before leaving the village to hunt, individuals would first visit the sweat lodge to prepare themselves. The Nez Perce believed that a strong body order was as offensive to animals as it was to people and that this would impair the success of the hunt. After cleansing themselves in the sweat lodge, the hunters would crush cottonwood leaves and rub these over their bodies as a rudimentary form of deodorant. Bathing and ritual cleansing of the body also prepared the warrior for combat or a woman for the successful gathering of camas roots.

## Cottontail Boy and Thunder

The importance of bathing as a precursor to successful action appears even in Nez Perce stories, including the story of Cottontail Boy. Cottontail Boy had stolen one of Thunder's wives, and he knew that Thunder would fight him to get her back. To prepare for the duel that lay ahead, he conditioned himself by bathing before their encounter. During the duel that ensued, Cottontail was able to avoid the thunderbolts and lighting thrown by Thunder, until an exhausted Thunder realized he had been beaten and conceded defeat to Cottontail. The sweat lodge, which is most often associated with Nez Perce ritual cleaning, also has a place in the stories of the tribe. In the time before humankind came into being, the sweat lodge, like the other features of the earth, was animated. It was the Sweat Lodge Man, or *Qi'wn*, who imparted the particular characteristics to the animals that inhabited the earth. However, after he had finished his task, Sweat Lodge Man did not disappear. Instead, he formed himself into the ground and vowed that all who came to him would be imparted with greater wisdom or skill in all things. While the bathing regimes of the Nez Perce are most often associated with male activities—all members of the tribe followed the same practices. Hot water baths were considered to be curative of disease, and both men and women would participate in them. Sweat baths were also used to cleanse an individual after exposure to someone who had died.

In Nez Perce beliefs, an individual's spirit could refuse to enter into eternity and remain earthbound. Invariably, these earthbound spirits would become malevolent and could curse the tribe or an individual as a whole. To encourage a spirit to move on, making earth less attractive to the departed spirit was paramount. In the sweat bath ritual, those who had been exposed to the corpse would cleanse themselves of the departed spirit. Cold-water bathing—especially in the ice-choked rivers of the high mountains—was thought to teach children how to endure hardship. As such, young children often stood in water, up to their necks, to develop the stamina and toughness they would need later in life. Bathing rituals, especially those involving children, were often performed with other tribal members in attendance to ensure the safety of all involved.

## GAMES FOR LIFE

Life for the Nez Perce was not only about the struggle to survive. Games and activities were common, and many were practiced to hone the skills an individual might need as an adult. Popular games included those that developed the dexterity and grace needed to fight and hunt. One such game was the pole race whereby an individual guided their horse as quickly as possible through a maze of poles that extended from the ground. This would improve an individual's skill in riding, which would prove to be a tremendous benefit during war or when hunting buffalo. Another popular game was to toss an object as close to a predetermined target as possible. Throwing games helped to develop the eye-hand coordination that was needed for hunting. For boys, wrestling would also help them to learn the skills of the warrior, should they ever find themselves in hand-to-hand combat.

While it was unusual for women to become warriors and hunters, their presence in war was not unheard of on the Columbia Plateau. Those who distinguished themselves would have been afforded the same privileges as male warriors and hunters. Girls most often mimicked the skills their mothers demonstrated when they wielded a knife to dress the meat that had been brought in from the hunt or to make the clothes and moccasins their people would wear.

All children learned the importance of the foods that grew in the country around them and learned how to harvest them in order to survive. While most children were engaged in the rough-and-tumble world of wrestling and merrymaking, a select few were not. These individuals had been designated, sometimes from birth, to be the leaders of their people. However, they would not become great warriors; instead, they would be the political leaders who guided their people in peace. Their training would be to observe the councils and learn all they could about the art of diplomacy and persuasion—an art they practiced from an early age when they were expected to be the mediators of disputes between their contemporaries. Joseph was designated to be just such an individual. The skills Joseph learned as a child and perfected as a young man served his people well when the Nez Perce were forced to deal with the white men who had settled in their territory.

## THE ENTRANCE OF THE WHITE MAN

The Nez Perce had not encountered any white men in their territory by the end of the 18th century, but that did not mean they remained unaffected by the encroaching foreign civilization. The Nez Perce and the other tribes of the Columbia Plateau experienced the devastating power of European diseases in a series of outbreaks during the course of the 18th century. In 1755 smallpox was introduced into the Columbia Plateau, and within a year's time, it had killed about 50 percent of the Nez Perce population, which numbered from 8,000 to 10,000 at that time. Unfortunately, the disease returned to wreak havoc on the native people of the region in 1760 and again in 1781.

However, not all the things introduced by the white man proved to be bad. The Nez Perce found that they had an affinity for the white man's horse. By the late 18th century, horses that had escaped from the herds brought over by the conquistadores to Mexico in the 16th century, and other horses that had escaped the hunters and trappers in the back woods of the north over the years, were traded to the tribes in the region. The Nez Perce obtained their first horses from the Shoshone and soon proved to be adept horse breeders and expert horsemen. So proficient were the Nez Perce in raising horses that when Meriwether Lewis allowed the Nez Perce to geld one of the horses used by the Corps, he noted, "I have no hesitation in declaring my belief that the Indian method of gelding is preferable to that practiced by ourselves."[5] The weaponry of the Euro-Americans was slower in arriving in the region, but stories of the power of the rifle in comparison to the bow and arrow had preceded the arrival of white settlers by almost a generation. It was into this world of the Nez Perce that a group of explorers would stumble, and their meeting would change history.

## NOTES

1. Lucullus Virgil McWhorter, *Yellow Wolf: His Own Story* (Caldwell, ID: Caxton Press, 2008), 18

2. William Clark and Meriwether Lewis, *Journals of the Lewis and Clark Expedition*, ed. Gary E. Moulton (Lincoln: University of Nebraska, 2003), 217.

3. Chief Joseph, *That All People May Be One People, Send Rain to Wash the Face of the Earth* (Kooskia, ID: Mountain Meadow Press, 1995), 3.

4. Ibid.

5. Clark and Lewis, *Journals of the Lewis and Clark Expedition*.

# Chapter 2

# THE CORPS OF DISCOVERY

## FIRST CONTACT

While the history of the Nez Perce Indians can be traced back thousands of years, they did not begin to occupy a place in American history until the beginning of the 19th century. What introduced them to America were a bedraggled group of men who in 1804 set out on an odyssey to map and explore the lands to the west of the Mississippi. Led by Captains Meriwether Lewis and William Clark, these 33 men would become known as the Corps of Discovery. The first meeting between the Nez Perce and the Corps occurred on September 20, 1805. After several exhausting days of travel over the Bitterroot Mountains, the Corps divided into two companies. The main company, led by Meriwether Lewis, traveled more slowly over the torturous, rocky paths; while a smaller company, led by William Clark, pushed ahead in the hope of meeting up with friendly Indians who would be able to assist them on the next leg of their journey, which would take them down the Columbia River.

After two days of searching the area, Clark and six men from the Corps entered Weippe Prairie in present-day Idaho and there encountered the Nez Perce Indians for the first time. In the windswept grasses of the prairie, two small bands of the Nez Perce had established their camps as part of their final journey from the lower valleys of the Columbia Plateau and into the protected mountain passes of the upper valleys where they would spend the winter. The bands had stopped in order to collect the camas roots that they would dry and then grind into flour to make bread. While the Indian women gathered the camas roots, most of the younger men left to hunt in the surrounding mountains or to take part in a raiding party against the Shoshone people in the south. The year before, the Shoshone had killed three Nez Perce emissaries who had been sent on a peace mission. None of the men were expected to return for two weeks. In their absence, the rest of the tribe would focus their attention on collecting food stores for the winter.

Since the season for harvesting the bounty from the earth was drawing to a close, the women were intent on their labors, hoping to collect as much as they could to help sustain their families through the long winter that lay ahead. With the women thus occupied and most of the men away from the camp, those who remained in the camp were young children or older people. Even the older children had quit the camp to play in the surrounding fields. Three of these boys would be the first to witness the entrance of the white man into their territory.

## The Entrance of the Dog Men

As they played, the boys caught a glimpse of something moving in the woods surrounding them. To their amazement, a man riding on horseback exited the woods, and he was soon joined by several other men. The sight of these strange men frightened the boys; they were filthy and smelled badly. All wore beards, and one had skin the color of night; he was Clark's slave, York. The boys had never seen a black man before, and the state and manner of the men assured them they were not from any of the neighboring tribes. The very strangeness of the men also made them look threatening, and as one of the boys would later remark, "They all had eyes like dead fish."[1] The now frightened boys hid in the tall grass and hoped the men would pass, but they were soon discovered and prevented from running away. However, instead of harming the boys, the men made gestures of peace and offered each of the boys a length of red ribbon. After several minutes of gesturing, it became apparent the strangers wanted to be introduced to the leaders of the Nez Perce band; once they had communicated this message, they released the boys to return to the village. The boys did as they were bidden and returned to their camp to report the strangers who were in their midst. After much discussion, it was decided that the strangers should be brought into the camp.

## The Soyapo

Once the strangers had entered the camp, the Indians gathered around them and saw at once that the boys' fanciful description of the strangers had not been wrong. Because of the hair on their faces, many within the village thought that these strangers might be descended from dogs. The villagers also noted the strangers carried guns. Since the introduction of Americans into the plains, word of these weapons had spread rapidly. However, the Nez Perce had never seen one of the weapons before, nor had they ever seen a white man. Clark and the men who were with him were led to a lodge in one of the camps and provided with food. They were informed that the great chief of the band was away, but that they would meet with another chief the following day. Satisfied with this explanation, Clark and his men, now well fed and feeling comfortable around these hospitable people, fell asleep in the lodge of the absent chief.

While they slept, a council was held to determine what should be done with them. While many were offended by the sight and smell of the strangers and felt they should be killed, one woman, *Wat-kue-is*, or "She Who Had Returned from a Far Country," spoke for the strangers and convinced the Nez Perce to allow them to live. Several years earlier, Wat-kue-is had been kidnapped by the Blackfeet Indians while her band hunted buffalo. She lived for a while with the Blackfeet but was subsequently sold to another Plains Indian tribe, and then sold again to a white man with whom she married and had a child. When her husband died, she left the white community she had been living in and made her way back to her people. During her sojourn with the people she came to call the *Soyapo*, or "Covered Ones," because of the hats they wore, she was treated kindly and grew very fond of them.

## The Decision to Spare Clark and His Men

The words of Wat-kue-is made a significant impression among the members of the band. With most of the men away hunting or at war, the very survival of the group could easily have been threatened by the arrival of these strangers. For the Nez Perce, their encounter with the dog men held a significantly different meaning than what Clark would surmise. The following day, the strangers were led to the camp of *Wala-mot-tinin,* or "Twisted Hair," who though old was still a respected chief among his people. Although he too was surprised by the look of these strange men, Twisted Hair treated them as honored guests and offered them a meal of buffalo meat, salmon, and camas bread. The strangers readily accepted his hospitality, and Clark noted in his journal that he found Twisted Hair to be a "chearfull man of about 65 with apparent sincerity."[2] After eating their fill, Clark explained why they had come into the land of the Nez Perce and was pleased to find that the Nez Perce were willing to assist them. On that second night, Clark and his men sat up until 1:00 in the morning smoking and talking with the old chief.

## Lewis's Entrance into the Nez Perce Camp

Two days after their initial contact with the Nez Perce, the rest of the Corps of Discovery, led by Lewis, entered the same valley. Lewis and Clark must have struck a pitiful pose for the Indians, the journey across the continent had been hard, and the men of the Corps of Discovery were tired and ailing. In their diary entries before meeting the Nez Perce, Lewis noted that the Corps' total provisions consisted of bear's oil and 20 pounds of beeswax candles. Unfortunately, the ample diet provided by the Indians to the near-starving members of the Corps of Discovery produced dysentery among the men, and several of them were unable to do anything but "lie on the Side of the road." By September 25, 1805, Clark noted in his journal that "Nearly all the men sick"[3] Lewis, the leader of the Corps of Discovery, was counted among those who were ill.

As the members of the Corps were unable to fully work to build the canoes they would need for their journey, they requested assistance from the Nez Perce in their construction and further information about the land they would cross as they completed their journey to the Pacific

Ocean. The Nez Perce readily proffered their assistance, giving the directions needed and showing Lewis and Clark's men how to use the natural grain of a tree to more easily carve the canoes they would use. While the nutritious and abundant food offered by the Nez Perce was partly responsible for the discomfort experienced by several of the men of the Corps of Discovery, it also undoubtedly saved many from further illness or possibly death.

## Clark Provides Medical Assistance to the Nez Perce

The willingness of the Indians to assist the ragged strangers earned them the praise of Clark, who wrote that the Indians showed them "greater acts of hospitality than we have witnessed from any nation or tribe since we have passed the rocky Mountains."[4] Eager to provide any possible kindness in return, Clark used his meager medical training to treat several of the Indians who complained of eye ailments. Since the Indians were preparing for their winter encampment, most now lived in elongated and enclosed houses, which trapped the smoke from their cooking fires and irritated their eyes. So proficient was he at providing relief that Clark's prowess as a healer spread rapidly through the camp. Despite struggling with illness, progress on the construction of the canoes continued, and by October 6, 1805, the canoes were ready for travel.

## Nez Perce Help the Explorers on Their Journey

Twisted Hair drew a map on the hide of an antelope skin that would lead the men to the Pacific Ocean. To ensure the Corps would be able to travel safely through the Columbia Plateau, Twisted Hair and another Nez Perce headman, *Teto-har-sky*, agreed to accompany the men as far as the great falls where the various tribes from the region gathered to trade before heading off to their winter camps. In the few weeks that Lewis and Clark stayed with the Indians, they found them to be "the likelyest and honestest we have seen and are verry friendly to us."[5]

Despite all the Indians had done to assist them at that pivotal juncture in their journey, Lewis and Clark had one more favor to request of the Nez Perce; they asked Twisted Hair to keep their horses and some equipment for them as they continued on their journey. With the same spirit of generosity that had earned the Nez Perce accolades from all members of the Corps, Twisted Hair agreed.

On October 7, Lewis and Clark pushed their canoes away from the banks of the Clearwater River, where Twisted Hair's village lay, and headed toward the west. As the company of men traveled toward the Columbia River and their final destination, the Pacific Ocean, they continued to enjoy assistance from the various bands of Nez Perce whose villages lined the rivers and tributaries. By October 16, the Lewis and Clark expedition finally entered the Columbia River and bid good-bye to the land of the Nez Perce. They would not return to the village of Twisted Hair until early May 1806.

## The Return of the Corps of Discovery

In the seven months they had been absent from Twisted Hair's village, their visit could have been forgotten, their horses appropriated, and any possessions they had abandoned long since distributed. However, when Lewis and Clark returned the following spring, they found their entire herd intact and well cared for and all of their possessions intact. Lewis and Clark's fame had spread during their absence, and when they reappeared, several prominent chiefs clamored to meet them, including the great war chiefs Neesh-ne-park-ke-ook, or "Cutnose," and Tunn-ache-moot-oolt, or "Broken Arm." Again Lewis and Clark were showered with hospitality and generously provided for by the Indians.

While they rested in the village of Broken Arm, more powerful war chiefs entered the encampment and met the Corps—Hohots-Ilppilp, or "Red Grizzly Bear"; Yom-park-kar-tim, or "Five Big Hearts"; and Apash Wyakaikt, or "Flint Necklace." The significance of these meetings would not be apparent at the time, however. Within a generation, the son of Twisted Hair, a chief who would be known as Hallalhootsoot, or Lawyer, would be pivotal in welcoming settlers into their homeland; and within two generations, the grandson of Flint Necklace, a war chief named Allalimya Takanin, or "Looking Glass," would help lead his people on the infamous flight from the U.S. Army in 1877. These great chiefs of the Nez Perce met in council to decide what to do with the returning explorers.

## The First Nez Perce Alliance

Each chief knew that the entrance of the Corps of Discovery would be only the first of many encounters with Americans in the future. Should they welcome the Soyapo into their lands or refuse them entry? Eventually, the chiefs determined "that the whiteman might be assured of their warmest attachment and that they would always give them every assistance in their power."[6] With the promise of a bright and peaceful future ahead, the members of the Corps of Discovery waited for the late winter snow to melt so they could be on their way.

While Lewis and Clark remained with Twisted Hair's people, they continued to enjoy the same friendly relations that had characterized their visit the previous year. Because of the success Clark had had treating members of the band for an eye ailment, several Indians approached

*A Nez Perce war chief, Looking Glass figured prominently in the Nez Perce conflict of 1877, directing the actions of his men against the pursuing U.S. Army. National Archives.*

him for assistance with a variety of complaints. Using the rudimentary medicines he had brought along, Clark was able to relieve most of the suffering of those who sought his care. Along with the medical services Clark provided, the men of the Corps also exchanged cultural information about themselves and the society from which they came.

### The "Book of Heaven"

Because the Nez Perce are a spiritual people, one aspect of their guests that interested them was their religious beliefs. Lewis and Clark were more than willing to explain their beliefs to the Nez Perce. Central to the Protestant religious beliefs of the Corps was the Holy Bible, and this they liberally read and shared with members of the tribe. To the Nez Perce, the Holy Bible became known as the "Book of Heaven." When the snows finally cleared and it was time for the Corps of Discovery to resume their journey, the Soyapo had increased in the estimation of the Nez Perce, and upon parting, they reiterated their oath to always be friends. Such was the auspicious beginning of the relationship between the people of the United States and the Nez Perce. Unfortunately, the good tidings would not last.

## FUR TRADERS FROM THE NORTH WEST COMPANY

The next contact the Nez Perce had with white Americans came quickly after Lewis and Clark left the Columbia Plateau. Drawn by the reports of abundant fur-bearing animals that lived along the rivers and streams of the region, trappers came into the area. The first large-scale attempt to establish a permanent base in the Columbia Plateau began in the summer of 1807 when David Thompson established a trading post on the bank of the upper Columbia River. While Thompson would abandon the region within the decade, the company he represented, the North West Company of Montreal, would remain in the region for several decades, which served as the impetus to draw still more trappers into the area.

By the 1820s, the British fur-trading companies had largely abandoned their attempts to control the trade in the Columbia Plateau, and the business of securing furs for trade fell almost exclusively to the Americans. Relations with these individuals and the Indians were peaceful for the most part but lacked the collegiality of the relationship that had developed between the men of the Corps of Discovery and the Nez Perce. The trappers were interested in only one thing—trading in the hides of animals. A few of them became friendly with the various bands of the Nez Perce, and some of the trappers were allowed to live and marry within the tribe, but for the most part, the relationship that developed was limited.

While Lewis and Clark had come to explore and record what they had seen, these men came purely to hunt and make a profit. To the Nez Perce, the single-minded pursuit of animals, solely to take their hides, was an affront to their Creator, who had provided the animals as a means of sustenance, not profit. Initially, they refused to assist the trappers in their hunting. In some instances, this led to animosity between the Nez Perce and the trappers; in other instances, to outright conflict. In the past, the Nez Perce might have been content to leave the trappers alone and to resume their daily sustenance activities. However, the trappers brought with them the guns and manufactured goods that the Indians wanted. The steel knives and guns were more effective than the knives made of flint or the bows and arrows the Indians had been using. The importance of these new weapons was significant; not only could they make a hunter more efficient, and thereby able to more adequately provide for his family, but they also could make the difference when war occurred between the various tribes in the plateau.

## Nez Perce Conflict and Accommodation among the Fur Traders

Unwilling to hunt merely to take the pelt of an animal, the Nez Perce instead established themselves as horse traders. Since the introduction of horses into the region in the early 18th century, the Nez Perce had proved themselves to be extraordinarily adept horsemen and breeders. The horses they bred were well known for their stamina and strength, something of which the trappers were in desperate need. However, the Nez Perce were also traders and understood that the value of a commodity increased along with its demand. When they raised the price of horses, very often this resulted in a hostile backlash from the trappers.

Rare incidences of violence erupted between the Nez Perce and the fur traders, but for the most part, trade was conducted peacefully.

Despite their reputation as horse breeders and their willingness to trade, the Nez Perce still did not enjoy access to all of the trade goods they wanted. To make matters worse, because they would not hunt merely for the pelts of animals, they were often unable to obtain the weapons they wanted, and the balance of power in the Columbia Plateau began to shift away from them. To regain their momentum, the Nez Perce decided to invite the Americans back into their lives by searching out what they believed to be the source of Lewis and Clark's power—their religion. However, in order to secure this information, it would be the Nez Perce who must travel to the land occupied by the Americans, instead of the other way around.

## THE HUDSON BAY COMPANY AND
## THE FIRST CONVERSION ATTEMPTS

While the Nez Perce had been curious about the religion of the members of the Corps of Discovery, their first prolonged exposure to the tenets of Christianity came a generation after Lewis and Clark had gone. In the early 1820s, the Hudson Bay Company, an English firm that hunted for furs in the Columbia Plateau, was ordered by the British government to provide religious instruction to the Indians living in the region. To accomplish this, several missions were "established at proper places for the conversion of the Indians."[7] By 1825 missionaries had convinced the Spokan and Kutenai Indians to allow them to raise two of their children in the religion of the white man.

Reluctantly, the chiefs of the respective tribes agreed to this, and each allowed one of their sons to accompany the missionaries back to their mission on the Red River in order to be educated in the ways of the white man. The boys were gone for three years, and when they returned, they spoke the white man's language and dressed and acted like the Soyapo. These boys also spoke about the mysteries of the Soyapo religion and began to instruct their people in its practice. News of the boys' return and of the stories they told spread rapidly throughout the region, and several bands of Indians from the Columbia Plateau, including the Nez Perce, came to hear the boys speak. After hearing the boys discourse about Christianity and the amazing things they had experienced within the Soyapo society, many came away amazed and awed.

## The Red River Mission

As a religious group of people, the Nez Perce had always been very accepting of the religious beliefs of other people, and many became convinced that the Soyapo had special knowledge about the wishes of the Creator because of the success of their society. Perhaps the fading influence of the Nez Perce in trade and in the power structures of the region could be reversed by tapping into the power offered by the religion of the white man. When the opportunity for additional boys to be educated at the Red River Mission school came available in 1830, five more boys from local tribes were selected to attend, including two who were from the Nez Perce tribe. One, named Ellis by the traders and whose Indian name has been lost, was the grandson of Hohots-Ilppilp, one of the powerful chiefs who had assisted Lewis and Clark on their return to the United States in 1806. The education of a few of their number, however, would not serve the needs of all of their people, so the Nez Perce sought a wider solution to their problem.

## THE DECISION TO ENTER THE LAND OF THE WHITE MAN

Several bands of the Nez Perce met in council to decide whether they would seek renewed contact with the Americans who had proved to be so friendly toward them a generation earlier. These bands came from the Kamiah Valley and included several of the powerful chiefs who had met Lewis and Clark on their return to the United States in 1806. The alliance that had been formed between Lewis and Clark was still fresh in the minds of many in the tribe. Reestablishing contact would give the Nez Perce access to the religious instruction they desired and would also potentially establish a trade route that would give them greater access to the manufactured goods of the white man.

Once the decision had been made to initiate contact, seven representatives were chosen, and the Nez Perce prepared to reenter the history of America. These men would travel to the great trade city of the Midwest, St. Louis. Because of the distance and their unfamiliarity with the route, the Nez Perce made arrangements with members of the American Fur Company to allow their delegates to accompany them when they returned to the city to obtain supplies for their men in the field.

In June 1831, just a scant year and a half since listening to the stories of the two boys who had returned from the Red River school, the Nez Perce were on their way. The journey would take four months. By the time the group had made its way to Council Bluff, Iowa, three of the Nez Perce delegates decided to turn back. By early fall, the four Nez Perce warriors, accompanied by their escorts from the American Fur Company entered into the city of St. Louis. The four Nez Perce men were *Tip-yah-lanah* (sadly the meaning of his name has been lost over time); *Hi-yuts-to-henin*, or "Rabbit Skin Leggings"; *Tawis Gee-jumnin*, or "No Horns on His Head"; and *Ka-ou-pu*, or "Man of the Morning."

## Nez Perce Warriors in St. Louis

Overwhelmed with the size and confusion of the city, the four Nez Perce warriors stayed close to their escorts and happily sought out anything familiar. The four Nez Perce warriors were taken to see William Clark, who in the 25 years since the Corps of Discovery had been in the Columbia Plateau had been promoted to general and was now the superintendent of Indian Affairs. When the Nez Perce delegates were taken to Clark's stately home on the corner of Vine and Market streets, hope of rekindling the friendship that had benefitted the Corps of Discovery was realized. During this second encounter with the Nez Perce, Clark was asked if he could arrange for someone to come to the Columbia Plateau to teach the Nez Perce about the white man's religion and the Bible.

## The Nez Perce Search
## for Religious Instruction

As the only connection the delegates had with America, Clark felt a sense of responsibility toward the Nez Perce and allowed them to stay in his home while they were in the city. His gesture of hospitality was well timed as the winter of 1831–1832 was so cold that the Mississippi River froze. Despite his hospitality, in the months that the four warriors spent in St. Louis, two of them died, *Tip-yah-lanah* on October 31 and *Ka-ou-pu* on December 17. Possibly their deaths were related to the extreme cold and unfamiliar surroundings in which they found themselves. Both men were buried in the graveyard of a local Catholic church.

By the early spring of 1832, the two surviving members of the Nez Perce delegation were ready to return home and await the missionary that had been promised them. Again accompanied by members of the American Fur Company, they left St. Louis on March 26 on board the steamship *Yellow Stone* and headed toward Fort Union in the Montana Territory. Each man had been given a "Book of Heaven," or Bible, to take back to their people to introduce them to the white man's religion.

Whether either man had been able to read any of the writings in the Bible is unknown; unfortunately, neither man ever made it home. *Tawis Gee-jumnin* died while on the steamship that carried the two warriors up the Missouri River and was buried at Fort Union. While *Hi-yuts-to-henin* was killed in a battle with the Blackfeet Indians as he approached the land of his people. While none of the four warriors were able to return safely home, stories of their exploits were passed from one band of Nez Perce to the next, and the purpose of their visit to St. Louis was realized.

## WILLIAM WALKER AND THE QUEST TO PROVIDE MISSIONARIES

While the Nez Perce had entered St. Louis to persuade the Americans to send missionaries to them in the Columbia Plateau, it was another Indian whose actions would bring their quest to fruition. While the Nez Perce delegates were in St. Louis, they caught the attention of a devout Methodist named William Walker.

Walker was a white man, but as a boy had been kidnapped by Delaware Indians and later traded to the Wyandot Indians. Walker lived among the Wyandot and eventually married a half-Wyandot woman named Catherine Rankin Walker who taught at the local mission school. In the years Walker had spent living among the Wyandot, he had become very influential in tribal affairs. Walker was actually in St. Louis on business for the Wyandot nation. The U.S. government wanted the tribe to exchange lands they had in Ohio for lands west of Missouri. Walker agreed to examine the proposed lands and was there that winter for that express purpose.

## Jason Lee and the Methodist Church

Walker went to visit the Indians who were staying at William Clark's house and came away impressed with their sincerity. On January 19, 1832, Walker penned a letter to a friend in New York, Gabriel Disoway, and expressed his hope that the Nez Perce be granted their wish. Disoway in turn published Walker's letter in the March 1831 editions of *The Christian Advocate and Journal* and *Zion's Herald*, a Methodist journal. Disoway called upon missionaries to grant the Nez Perce their request. Because of his persistence, by 1834 the Methodist Church dispatched the Reverend Jason Lee to the Pacific Northwest to establish the mission the Nez Perce had requested.

Jason Lee was born in 1803, in Stanstead, Quebec, a small town nestled along the border between the United States and Canada; Lee was a powerfully built man who seemed perfectly suited for the rigors of life in the untamed Northwest. Lee had already spent the past several years preaching to the Indians and whites who lived along the national borders of the two countries, and when offered the opportunity to extend his mission into the Northwest, Lee readily agreed to lead four other Methodist missionaries into the Nez Perce country. They included his nephew, Daniel Lee; Cyrus Shepard, who proved to be wholly unable to adapt to life in the wilderness; Courtney Walker; and Philip Walker.

Despite being dispatched to tend to the religious needs of the Nez Perce, the rough and unfamiliar life of the wilderness prompted the men to take the advice of Nathaniel Wyeth, a trapper who guided them into the region, and to settle in the Willamette Valley, an area that was outside Nez Perce territory. Wyeth argued, and the missionaries agreed, that this area gave them greater access to the supplies they would need to survive and to fulfill their mission. Once in the valley, they established a school along the Willamette River to educate the Indians. However, their efforts were met with little success. Shepard was so overwhelmed by the task before him that he often isolated himself away from the mission and spent hours weeping in misery.

## Early Missionary Failures

In 1835, the first year the school was open, the missionaries had 14 students; of those, 7 died and another 5 ran away during the first year. The following year, the missionaries could count 25 students at the school, but of those, 16 fell ill and only 1 actually converted to Christianity. Jason Lee, as many of the other missionaries who would follow him, had entered into the arena of Christianizing the Indians of the Columbia Plateau with the mind-set that in order for the Indians to become Christians, they must first abandon their "wild and uncivilized" culture and traditions. To exact that change, those individuals placed under Lee's control were forced to wear white man's clothes, cut their hair, and learn to read and write English. Only then could the "heathen" Indians become Christians.

Lee's attitude toward his charges was also peppered by contempt. Lee came to consider himself as culturally, religiously, and morally superior to the Indians in the region and recommended to those missionaries who followed him to "let not the Indians trifle with you, let them know that you must be respected, and whenever they intentionally transgress bounds, make them feel the weight of your displeasure."[8] It is with little wonder then that Lee experienced difficulty in enticing the Indians of the Columbia Plateau to his mission. The number of deaths reported in the first years of his mission only served to confirm to the Nez Perce that the mission did not accurately reflect what they believed was the true teaching of the "Book of Heaven."

While the Indians were interested in religious instruction, the schools also became a breeding ground for disease. Crowded into enclosed spaces for hours on end and exposed to new foods and cultural practices that did not reflect the level of cleanliness they enjoyed in their traditional environment, many of the students fell ill. Parents watched in horror as their children died from these diseases, and they subsequently limited their support for the schools. Because of his limited success and contempt for the Indians he had been sent to Christianize, Lee came under criticism from several of the other missionaries who came into the region, many of whom called for his removal.

For the next 10 years, Lee was the head of missionary activity in the region but after a few years seemed to lose interest in his primary mission and instead focused on moving white settlers into the region and laying the groundwork for the establishment of a provisional government in the Oregon Territory. Because of his limited success in converting the Indians, his poor standing among other missionaries, and his focus on establishing a government within the territory, the Methodist Church replaced him in 1843. Stung by the criticism leveled at him by his contemporaries, Lee would spend the next two years trying to clear his name of any wrongdoing; his efforts ended with his death in 1845.

## BEGINNING OF THE WHITMAN AND SPALDING MISSIONS

Because of Lee's failure, direct missionary activity among the Nez Perce Indians would not begin until the arrival of Dr. Marcus and Narcissa Whitman, and Henry and Eliza Spalding in 1836. While the devotion of each couple to their religion cannot be denied, each had fatal flaws that would hinder their ability to effectively minister to their Indian charges. Narcissa Prentiss-Whitman, while beautiful and intelligent, was also aloof and reserved when dealing with the Indians. She and Henry Spalding also did not like each other, and this would hamper their ability to effectively complete their mission.

Henry Harmon Spalding was a man with a troubled past; born out of wedlock, he had been raised in a foster home and as a young man seemed destined to live his life in dissolution and waste. However, when he was 22, Spalding experienced a religious conversion and wholly embraced his newfound life. Eventually, his zealous embrace of religion would lead him into missionary work. However, Spalding also proved to be inflexible in his attitudes toward others, and those who earned his enmity usually kept it. Narcissa Whitman was one of those people.

Dr. Marcus Whitman originally had hoped to study theology and become a minister; however, finances and time prevented him from accomplishing his goal. Instead, he apprenticed himself to an experienced physician and entered into Fairfield Medical College. Once he had completed his two years of study, he applied to become a missionary. However, of the requirements imposed on missionaries at that time, one insisted they be married. The still single Marcus was again denied the opportunity to fulfill his life's ambition. In 1835 Marcus met Narcissa Prentiss; when the two discovered they shared the same goal of missionary work, they quickly married and applied to become missionaries to the Nez Perce.

The last of the missionaries was Eliza Hart-Spalding. Eliza was described as serious and stubborn; yet of the two couples, she developed the greatest rapport with the Indians. She quickly learned their language and devoted herself to their education, both in the rudiments of reading and writing, and religion. Eliza Spalding understood that teaching all the Nez Perce the English language would not be possible, and so she painstakingly compiled an alphabet in the Nez Perce language, which would eventually be used by her husband to write religious tracts to aid in the conversion of the Nez Perce people. Her willingness to learn more about the people she had come to minister to would eventually save her life.

## The Waiilatpu and Lapwai Missions

The Whitmans established their mission along the Walla Walla River at a place called *Waiilatpu* and primarily served the Cayuse people. Unfortunately for the Whitmans, they established their mission on land that had been claimed by a respected chief of the Cayuse named *Umtippe*, or "Split Lip." Unable or unwilling to consider that the Indians had a concept of land use that differed from their own, the Whitmans were confused by the reaction of the Cayuse when they established their mission. The issue was resolved a short time later when the elderly Umtippe died and thereby relinquished his claim to the land, but the damage had already been done.

The Spaldings established their mission near a Nez Perce village called *Lapwai*, or "The Place of the Butterfly." This land was claimed by the headman *Hin-mah-tute-ke-kaikt*, or "Thunder Eyes," although the white settlers in the region would come to know him by his Christian name, James. The two new missions were allowed to be built with the agreement that annual payments would be made to the tribe to make up for the loss of their land. This agreement was not kept.[9] This new batch of missionaries held many of the same cultural beliefs that had plagued Lee and relegated him to failure.

Missionaries believed that their goal was to not only convert the Indians to Christianity, but also to civilize them. Since the Indians moved seasonally to collect the food they needed to sustain themselves,

Americans believed that native culture was inferior to their own. They believed settled farming was a mark of civilization since it indicated permanence and commerce. Additionally, the missionaries mistakenly believed that the Indians had no culture or law because they did not have a written language and sought to impose their culture and laws upon the Indians they encountered. Initially, these new missionaries were welcomed into the region and enjoyed some success. However, their success at Christianizing some of the Nez Perce would eventually act as a wedge between the traditional Nez Perce who rejected Christianity and the growing white community.

## Cultural Clash at the Lapwai Mission

In 1837 a cultural clash occurred when the assumptions of Henry Spalding conflicted with the cultural beliefs of the Nez Perce. Spalding believed that the Nez Perce would need to settle into being farmers and ranchers in order to be civilized and to accept Christianity. Subsequently, he determined the Indians must focus less on raising horses and more on raising cattle. In order for his plan to work, however, Spalding needed to convince several of the leading chiefs of the Nez Perce to give him a number of horses that could be traded in the United States for the needed cattle. Spalding eventually prevailed in his argument by reckoning that the cattle could replace the buffalo the Indians hunted.

Since the hunting of buffalo required great skill on the part of the hunter and was not without its dangers, the chiefs agreed. Spalding gave the task of driving the horses to market and returning with the cattle to another young missionary, William Gray. He also convinced four Nez Perce men to assist Gray in his task. Among the four were two Nez Perce chiefs, Ellis and Blue Cloak. Ellis had been educated at the mission in Red River, spoke English, and knew the customs of the Americans. He had been back among his people for four years when Spalding directed him to assist in the livestock exchange.

When Ellis and Blue Cloak returned to Lapwai several months later because their horses were too fatigued to travel farther, Spalding was incensed. He condemned both men for refusing to follow his orders and for leaving Gray with only a minimal escort. Spalding then ordered the two men given 50 lashes and demanded they pay him a fine of a horse each. Ellis refused to comply with Spalding's demand and left the area, but Blue Cloak did not believe Spalding was serious in his threat and later came to the mission for church service. Spalding ordered other Nez Perce men to seize Blue Cloak and to whip him.

One young warrior, *Tonwitakis*, seized Blue Cloak and tied his hands but insisted that Spalding do the whipping. Spalding refused to take up the whip and insisted that he "stood in the place of God" and as such "I command."[10] Spalding's imperious statement did little to compel Tonwitakis or other Nez Perce to follow his order. When Spalding still refused to carry out the punishment he had prescribed, Tonwitakis insisted that if he did not, the Nez Perce would whip Spalding. Unable to get the Indians to follow his bidding, Spalding eventually complied and whipped Blue Cloak for his transgression. Spalding also succeeded in forcing Blue Cloak to give him a horse. Spalding's insistence on the punishment and his disregard for the authority of Chief Blue Cloak resulted in increased tension between the Nez Perce and the missionary. Additional incidents like this one withdrew Nez Perce support for Spalding's mission and almost ended the endeavor.

## Disagreement among the Missionaries

In addition to the issues between the Indians and the missionaries, the missionaries themselves fell into backbiting, which only increased the tension in the area and made it difficult for the Indians to seriously consider the missionaries' message. Despite the problems experienced and caused by the missionaries, many Indians in the Columbia Plateau would consent to join the Christian Church. One such individual who came under the influence of Henry Spalding's mission was the political leader of the *Wellamotkin* band of Nez Perce, a man named *Tuekakas*.

After his arrival in the land of the Nez Perce, Spalding had only sporadic success with his conversion efforts. Several Indian chiefs had quarreled with Spalding, and by 1839, he would confide in his diary that he felt "discouraged" by his lack of success.[11] For almost a year, neither he nor Marcus Whitman had baptized a single Indian into the church. Desperate to show some success for his efforts, Spalding made a trip into the Wallowa Valley in midsummer to assess the religious progress of some of the Indians there.

## The Conversion of Tuekakas:
## Chief Joseph's Father

In particular, Spalding's attention was drawn to Tuekakas. In the few years he had lived among the Nez Perce, Spalding had made several missteps, but he found Tuekakas to be sincere in his interest and devotion to Christianity. In December 1838, Tuekakas had assisted Spalding in conducting a service and noted with great satisfaction that the Indian was very effective in moving his fellow tribal members toward Christianity. Satisfied that Tuekakas was ready for baptism, Spalding baptized him and other members of his band into the church in November 1839.

To mark his baptism, Spalding assigned Tuekakas an English name, Joseph. However, to more clearly separate him from his son, he is most often called "Old Joseph." Spalding married Old Joseph and his wife, *Khap-kha-pon-imi*, in the church and assigned her the name Asenath to mark her acceptance into Christian society. A week after the marriage of the parents, Spalding baptized their children.

So zealous was Spalding in obtaining converts that he claimed to have baptized four children that belonged to Old Joseph and Khap-kha-pon-imi; however, the Nez Perce only acknowledged the couple had two children at the time. It is possible that Spalding baptized individuals who were related to Old Joseph as there was little distinction made between individuals who were cousins, and each routinely would have called themselves brothers and sisters. From this misunderstanding comes the belief that Young Joseph had an older brother named *Sou-Sou-Quee* who died sometime in the mid-1860s at the hands of other Indians.

Spalding's decision to baptize Old Joseph was questioned by other missionaries in the area and served as one of the greatest complaints they had against Spalding and his conversion efforts. Other white missionaries, including Marcus Whitman and Elijah White, believed that he had acted prematurely and that Old Joseph was not ready to make a commitment to the church. Undaunted by the criticism, Spalding pressed on with his efforts. Over the next year, Spalding and his flagging mission would enjoy the support of Old Joseph and his people.

**Baptism of Chief Joseph.** While the Nez Perce would largely rebuff Spalding's attempts to turn them into farmers, they supported his efforts to bring converts into the church. To Spalding's delight, on April 12, 1840, he had the privilege of baptizing another of Old Joseph's children. This child, whom Spalding called Ephraim, would grow up to be Chief Joseph; however, among his people he was called *In-mut-too-yah-lat-lat*. More than a year after Joseph's baptism, his brother *Ollokot*, or "Frog," would also be baptized at the Spalding mission.

Young Joseph and his brother were afforded privileges that other Nez Perce children were denied. Their father's position as a leader of his people and as a recent convert to Christianity literally opened the door of the schoolhouse to them. Young Joseph learned to write his name and began the rudiments of a formal education at the Lapwai Mission school. Joseph and his brother and sisters were also allowed to play with the young children of the missionaries. This gave them an intimate glimpse into the world of the white man, something that would guide Young Joseph as he grew into manhood and began the task of leading his people.

***Spalding's Influence over Chief Joseph's Family.***   In addition to the education and baptism of Old Joseph, Spalding's influence extended well into Old Joseph's extended family. Old Joseph's father had been a Cayuse chief, and his mother came from the Kallapoon band of the Nez Perce. However, the match between his parents was not a good one, and before Old Joseph was born, his mother left the Cayuse and returned to her own people. Old Joseph was raised among the Nez Perce, but he retained a family connection to the Cayuse.

As word of Spalding's activities spread, individuals from surrounding tribes began arriving at the mission. One occasional visitor was *Pahkatos Qoh Qoh*, or "Five Crows," Old Joseph's half brother. Five Crows was eventually given the name Hezekiah by Spalding when he was baptized into the church. Unfortunately for Spalding, his success at baptizing Old Joseph and many members of Old Joseph's band did not lead to a softening of his attitudes toward the Indians or his insistence that they wholeheartedly embrace the white culture.

To those Indians who accepted his religious and cultural instruction, Spalding was stern and autocratic, but to those "heathen" Indians who refused to accept his proposals, he had little but contempt.[12] This contempt was only exacerbated by the influx of other missionaries and settlers into the region and eventually led to competition for the land. The non-Christian Indians resented the presence of the missions on their lands and destroyed or stole property as a way to force out the intruders. Spalding and the other white settlers demanded redress for such incursions but saw little wrong with their own actions.

## INFLUENCE OF THE
## CATHOLIC MISSIONARIES

The issues surrounding the belief in their own cultural superiority and prejudice against the Indians they had been called to serve would not be the only problem the Protestant missionaries would have in the Columbia Plateau. Catholic missionaries also entered the region with instruction to "take possession of those various places in the name of the Catholic religion."[13] At the time, relations between Catholics and Protestants were marred by intolerance and prejudice. This animosity spilled over into the efforts to bring Christianity to the Indians in the region.

When Catholic priests arrived in the Columbia Plateau in 1837, they set about undoing much of the work that had been done by the Protestant missionaries; the priests insisted the missionaries were "false teachers" and rebaptized and remarried those Indians who had already been married and accepted into the Protestant churches.[14] With each religious group vying for converts, both groups liberally criticized each other and attempted to undermine each other's progress in obtaining converts. To counter the growing number of Protestant missions being established in the area, the Catholic Church opened its first church in Champoeg in 1836, although it would not officially be consecrated by a priest for another three years because the missionary activity in the plateau prevented a priest from being permanently assigned there.

For the Indians who witnessed this infighting, the childish behavior of the Protestant and Catholic missionaries negated the message of tolerance and love that was supposed to be at the heart of the Christian religion and convinced many of the Indians to avoid the missionaries and their message. Others joined one religious group, and then another, like James, the Nez Perce chief on whose land Henry Spalding built his mission, who first accepted Protestantism and then, according to William Gray, had been convinced to "receive a cross and a string of beads."[15] Others like Old Joseph remained loyal to the missionaries they had originally encountered. Despite the growing conflict between the missionaries themselves and between missionaries and the Indians they were called to serve, more came into the region to establish the schools and missions that were central to their purpose.

## THE KAMIAH AND CLATSOP MISSIONS

Marcus Whitman and Henry Spalding were not the only missionaries in the Willamette Valley. By 1839 Asa B. Smith had established the Kamiah Mission, and the following year, Joseph H. Frost established the Clatsop Mission. However, one of the more influential men to enter the region was Dr. Elijah White. In 1836 Dr. Elijah White and his family were assigned to assist Jason Lee in his missionary efforts. After an arduous journey that took them almost a year, White, his wife, and two young sons arrived in the Oregon Territory in May 1837.

### Elijah White and Conflict
### at the New Missions

Unfortunately for the Indians they had been sent to serve, Lee and White could not have been more different from each other. Almost immediately, they set to quarreling with each other over how each believed the mission should be run and over relations with the Indians. Eventually, their quarrels grew more heated, and in 1841 White was forced to resign from the mission under a cloud of suspicion that he had misdirected funds intended for the Indians and had been inappropriate with several native women. However, White was not content to remain in the East and let matters lie.

After his return to the East, he approached the federal government and established himself as an expert on the Oregon Territory and its inhabitants and requested appointment as the governor of the territory. Since the Oregon Territory at that time was jointly occupied by both the United States and Great Britain, no such appointment was forthcoming as it would have been tantamount to the United States claiming the territory outright. Undeterred, White continued to push and was eventually commissioned as an Indian subagent for the region. Triumphant, White headed back to Oregon in 1842 with his new appointment in hand and more than 100 new settlers for the plateau.

White's appointment effectively placed him in a commanding position over Jason Lee and the other missionaries and established him as the highest ranking U.S. government official in the area. White used his newfound authority to impose his will on the Indians by issuing a series of regulations that would penalize the Indians in any dispute with white men and only succeeded in irrevocably damaging relations between the two groups.

White's actions were extremely controversial since control of the Oregon Territory had not been assumed by either the United States or Great Britain; each nation agreed only to jointly occupy the same land. When White established his rules of conduct, he was effectively extending U.S. authority over the region and over the native people who resided there, none of whom recognized the authority of any government over them, except their own. Most of the regulations imposed by White were one sided and applied only to the Indians; the regulations also sharply contrasted with how relations between the federal government and Native Americans had been conducted up to that time.

In dealing with the native people that inhabited the United States, the federal government had regulated relations between whites and Indians through a series of treaties. These treaties generally stipulated that each group would inhabit a specific area and that peace would prevail between the Americans and the Indians. White, however, stepped outside this model and instead established with his code of conduct a more autocratic and less collegial relationship with the tribes. While White possibly intended to stave off the increasing animosity that was growing between the settlers and the Indians, his autocratic and arrogant regulations only added fuel to the fire.

## The Appointment of Ellis as the High Chief of the Nez Perce

In order to make communication between the newly established federal government (White) and the Indians more convenient and to ensure that the Indians were held accountable for their actions, White also determined that the Nez Perce should elect among themselves a "high chief of the tribe"[16] to whom all other bands and chiefs would be subordinate. This new high chief would be responsible to the settlers for the enforcement of the regulations. When the confused Nez Perce advised they were unable to choose a single leader among themselves, White appointed the now 32-year-old Christianized grandson of Hohots-Ilppilp, Ellis, to be the new high chief.

The appointment of Ellis garnered much resentment among the Nez Perce. He was too young to have distinguished himself among his people in either war or in diplomacy. When Ellis attempted to impose his will on the older chiefs, including Old Joseph, they merely ignored him. White's heavy-handed decree and choice of Ellis as an appointed leader of the Nez Perce widened the fracture that had been growing between the Indians and the white settlers in their territory. By 1843 attempts to enforce White's code of conduct broke down when the tribal chiefs refused to comply with its mandates. Additionally, rumors abounded that Marcus Whitman, who had recently left for the East, had gone to secure support from the U.S. Army for a war against the tribes of the Columbia Plateau or that he would bring new settlers to take their lands. White's code of conduct came at an inauspicious time in the Willamette Valley, and his actions would lead to tragedy for both the settlers and the Indians in the region.

## RAPID CHANGE IN THE NORTHWEST

By the opening of the 1840s, the fur trade in the area had collapsed, and the region was riddled with men who no longer had the means to support themselves. Destitute, many wandered through the region in a desperate search for the once seemingly inexhaustible animals they had hunted. Unable to support themselves, several took to stealing from the Indians or white settlers and then blamed the Indians for their conduct. In addition to this increase in crime and social dislocation, competition from the Catholic missionaries challenged the authority of the Protestant missionaries.

Elijah White's code of conduct and his single-handed introduction of more than 100 new settlers into a region that was already beginning to show the strains of overcrowding only added to the turmoil. However, White's return to the Columbia Plateau would prove to be equally as disruptive to the missions of the Whitmans and the Spaldings. While he had been in the East, he had approached the American Board of

Commissioners for Foreign Missions and complained bitterly about the antics of Whitman and Spalding and of their inefficiency in securing converts to Christianity. So damning was his criticism that the board elected to recall both Spalding and Whitman and close the missions in the Northwest. When White returned to the Oregon Territory, he brought with him the message of their dismissal.

## Recall of Henry Spalding

The decision of the board to recall Henry Spalding came just when the Lapwai Mission seemed on the verge of success. With the assistance of Old Joseph and another powerful chief, *Tamootsin*, or Timothy, the mission had begun to show progress. The mission school boasted an enrollment of about 85 Indians, including "six of whom are chiefs and principal men."[17] Unwilling to give in without a fight, Marcus Whitman immediately returned to the East to plead with the board to keep the missions open; his efforts were successful. Whitman insisted that it was difficult to both convert the Indians to Christianity and assimilate them into white culture with the limited number of settlers in the area. Subsequently, when Whitman returned to the Pacific Northwest in the spring of 1843, he brought with him 1,000 new settlers.

Whitman's introduction of new settlers heralded even greater numbers to follow. In 1844 another 500 settlers entered the region, and the following year, 3,000 more would follow. By 1846 another 1,500 settlers swelled the already burgeoning ranks of those who had made their way along the Oregon Trail to enter the Oregon Territory. The swelling ranks of settlers were drawn to the rich soil of the Willamette Valley and spurred by recent political events in America. In 1845 James Polk became the new president of the United States. As an expansionist, Polk believed that Americans had an almost divine right to assume control of all of the land that encompassed the continental United States.

## Manifest Destiny and the Struggle
## for the Land

This idea would become known as *manifest destiny*, and Americans showed support for the idea by taking control of new and ever-expanding swaths of territory. When an agreement with Great Britain was reached that ceded the Oregon Territory to the United States, a new provisional government under the direction of George Abernathy was established. To the Indians in the Columbia Plateau, it seemed as if their fears were accurate; the Americans intended to seize their land and challenge their sovereignty. The introduction of so many new settlers, the imposition of a foreign and unrecognized government, and the autocratic and misguided actions of men like Elijah White produced enough chaos within the region to undo much of the work that the missions could previously boast. Additionally, those Indians who had previously supported the missionaries and who were attempting to live a settled agricultural life were harassed by non-Christian Indians until most abandoned their efforts.

By 1846 missionary efforts at Kamiah were suspended because so few Indians continued to support the mission. Many of the previous converts openly taunted the missionaries by returning to their traditional ways and shamans. Fence rails that had been carefully hammered into the ground to corral the mission livestock were torn out of the ground and used for firewood, and the animals were slaughtered and consumed in feasts.

In the fall of 1845, a group of Nez Perce traditionalists held a dance outside the Lapwai Mission. When Spalding protested their actions, he was seized and thrown into the fire. Spalding was saved from serious injury because of the heavy buffalo robe he was wearing, but the message sent by the Nez Perce was unmistakable. He was no longer welcome to live among them. Spalding, however, refused to leave, and vandalism against the mission building and insults directed at both Spalding and his wife became commonplace. As the hostility escalated, misunderstanding increased, which would lead to tragedy for both the Indians and the missionaries.

## GROWING HOSTILITIES BETWEEN THE INDIANS AND SETTLERS

By 1847 relations between the Indians of the Columbia Plateau and the white settlers reached an all-time low. The influx of so many settlers into the region added one last element to the simmering caldron—disease. Because they had lived remotely from white settlements for so long, the native people of the Pacific Northwest did not enjoy the same immunity to disease that the settlers who entered their territory did. Because of their lack of previous exposure, the Indians quickly succumbed to a variety of new diseases. Attempts by the Whitmans and Spaldings to assist the Indians failed miserably. Because the missionaries were either unscathed or suffered only mild eruptions of the diseases, many of the Indians became convinced that the missionaries were actually witches and had intentionally inflicted the diseases upon them in order to steal their lands.

The idea that the missionaries were witches was not new. In 1839 Narcissa Whitman had tended to two sick Indian children while her husband was away. She gave one of them medicine, but the child later died. The child's death was blamed on her, and she was branded a witch by the local tribe. While the incident eventually died down, resentment and fear of the unfamiliar ways of the missionaries continued to fester. To compound the problems with disease, the winter of 1846–1847 proved to be a particularly hard one. This left the Indians with few food reserves from which to draw, and the poor weather shortened the time they would have to gather the food they would need for the following year. This meant that the potential for a winter in which many could starve was very real. However, as the Nez Perce and the other tribes of the Columbia Plateau began to gather the food they would need, a steady and seemingly unrelenting stream of white settlers invaded their lands and challenged them for the limited resources. The year 1847 saw the largest influx of immigrants to date; between 4,000 and 5,000 entered the fertile valleys and took for themselves the food the Indians needed to survive.

## THE MASSACRE AT THE WAIILATPU MISSION

Additional rumors that Marcus Whitman and Henry Spalding had devised a plan to poison the Indians in order to seize their land also began to spread. This baseless rumor was fueled by an unlikely source, a half white and half Nez Perce Indian named Joe Lewis, who had traveled from Maine to assist the Whitmans at the Waiilatpu Mission. With the medicine of Marcus Whitman seemingly ineffective against the diseases

that ravaged the native population, Lewis's rumor began to gain cre-
dence. As the summer gave way to winter, resentment on the part of the
Indians ran high and resulted in one of the seminal tragedies in the
movement to settle the West. On November 29, the Cayuse and Umatilla Indians attacked the Whitman Mission and killed 13 missionaries,
including Marcus and Narcissa Whitman.

The massacre, while shocking and tragic, did not appear to be a sur-
prise to the missionaries, least of all the Whitmans. In the days preceding the attack, Marcus and Narcissa Whitman continued their work at
the mission, which was crowded with people who had come to settle in
the Oregon country. The Indians they had come so far to serve were largely
absent. Nevertheless, Marcus Whitman continued to make rounds into
the Indian villages to treat the victims of the measles outbreak. Whitman finished his rounds on the evening of November 28 and returned to
the mission late in the evening. On his rounds, Whitman heard the rumors that the Cayuse Indians were planning an attack on the Waiilatpu Mission and meant to kill both him and Narcissa. Despite the
warning, and despite feeling a sense of impending doom, Whitman did
nothing to ensure the safety of his family or the other 72 people who
resided at the mission.

The next afternoon at about 2:00 P.M., the attack began, innocuously
enough when the Cayuse chief *Tilokaikt* approached Marcus Whitman
at his home and requested medicine. While Whitman busied himself
with the chief's request, a second Indian named *Tomahas* hit Whitman
over the head with a tomahawk. Whitman was not immediately killed,
but this assault served as a signal to other Indians to begin a wider attack
of the mission. As the Indians fired their weapons into the mission buildings, Narcissa's arm was struck by a bullet and as she struggled to recover,
she was pulled outside and then shot repeatedly until she died. In the
attack, which flared up and died out many times over the next several
days, 11 more whites would be killed by the Indians, and 3 more would
die from disease or while trying to escape.

To compound the terror experienced by the residents of the mission,
47 were held as captives. The mission buildings were then looted and
burned to the ground. The attack on the Waiilatpu Mission was intended
to be only the first in a series of attacks that would push the missionaries
and the settlers out of the Columbia Plateau. Whitman and Spalding

had been targeted for annihilation first for several reasons: the influx of settlers that followed their entrance among the Indians, their autocratic behavior toward the Indians they served and their attempts to destroy the fundamental aspects of the native cultures they had encountered, and the rumors of their complicity in spreading disease among the Indians.

When the massacre at the Waiilatpu Mission was complete, Henry Spalding was in considerable peril. However, unfortunately, he was completely unaware that he was in any danger. Spalding had accompanied Marcus Whitman on his rounds through the Indian villages on the day before the massacre but had injured himself in a fall from his horse. Unable to return to the mission with Whitman, Spalding instead remained as a guest in the lodge of Five Crows, or Hezekiah, who lived near the village of Tilokaikt along the Umatilla River. When Tilokaikt confessed the attack to a visiting priest, Father John Baptiste Brouillet, the following day, word of the massacre began to enter into the consciousness of the white community.

## The Rescue and Protection of Henry and Eliza Spalding

Amazingly, Spalding remained ignorant of the attack and of the danger he faced until two days later when he came upon Father Brouillet as he left Tilokaikt's village. In desperation, Spalding fled into the countryside and attempted to make his way toward the Lapwai Mission and his own family. For several days, Spalding hid from his pursuers and alternately made his way toward the mission. When he finally got within sight of the mission, his heart sank; the entire area seemed to be filled with Indians. As he stared in disbelief, a Nez Perce woman saw Spalding and hurried down into the encampment to notify the others there. Several Indians, led by a Christianized Indian named Luke, found Spalding, protected him, and reassured him that his wife and children were safe.

On the day of the massacre, several of the residents at the Waiilatpu Mission escaped and were able to alert the military forces at Fort Walla Walla. One of those survivors was William Canfield, who stumbled into the Lapwai Mission with a bullet in his hip and revealed the awful truth of the massacre to Eliza Spalding. However, instead of fleeing into the countryside in a panic, she trusted the Indians who had been loyal to her and found protection in the camp of Hin-mah-tute-ke-kaikt, or James, the shaman who had allowed the Spaldings to build their mission on his land a dozen years earlier.

While Spalding enjoyed the protection of the Christianized Indians who had remained loyal to both him and his wife, the Cayuse and other bands of Nez Perce and Umatilla Indians still sought to harm him. It was only through the efforts of the Christianized Indians that he was saved. As Spalding surveyed the ruins of the Lapwai Mission, he saw several Indians among the looters who he believed were from Old Joseph's band. However, if this were true, Old Joseph was not party to the destruction of the mission, and Young Joseph continued to insist until the end of his life that when his father died, "there was no stain on his hands of the blood of a white man."[18] The following day, Spalding was reunited with his wife and children.

Concerned with a wider Indian uprising, the settlers in the surrounding communities decided against a general war to answer the attack. Instead, they would focus their attention on those who had actually committed the atrocities. The survivors of the massacres were forced to endure several more weeks of uncertainty before their rescue was secured in the last days of December. Once their safety was ensured, the settlers sought their revenge against the Cayuse, but, as often happened, the settlers made little distinction between those Indians who had taken part in the attack and those who had not.

## Aftermath of the Attack on the Missions

Faced with the increasing influx of white settlers into their lands, the devastation of disease, the autocratic behavior of a government whose legitimacy the Nez Perce did not recognize, and the imposition of an unfamiliar government over them, the Indians in the Columbia Plateau longed to reclaim their lands and return to their old ways. Convinced that the white man was evil, in 1848 the Cayuse entered into what became known as the Cayuse War. While many of the settlers, including Henry Spalding, believed Old Joseph had turned against them and had joined in the hostilities, there is no evidence to support the contention that he had.

Eventually, five Cayuse chiefs were tried and executed for the massacre. However, the mistrust between the settlers and their former friend continued to deteriorate until Old Joseph had decided he had had enough of the white man's ways, and instead of fighting with them over his land and the government of his people, he chose instead to return to the Wallowa Valley and to the traditions of his people. In was in the Wallowa Valley that Young Joseph would grow to manhood, and from there he would lead his people on their infamous flight from the authority of the American government.

## NOTES

1. Kent Nerburn, *Chief Joseph and the Flight of the Nez Perce* (San Francisco: Harper Collins, 2006), 4.

2. Meriwether Lewis and William Clark, *The Journals of the Lewis and Clark* (Whitefish, MT: Kessinger Publishing, 2004), 199.

3. Ibid., 202.

4. Reuben Gold Thwaites, ed., *Original Journals of the Lewis and Clark Expedition, Volume 5, Parts 1&2 Digital On* (Scituate, MA: Digital Scanning, 2002), 18.

5. Clark and Lewis, *Journals of the Lewis and Clark Expedition*, 219.

6. Meriwether Lewis and William Clark, "Journal Entry, May 12, 1806," *lewisandclarkjournals*, http://lewisandclarkjournals.unl.edu/.

7. Alvin M. Josephy, Jr. *The Nez Perce Indians and the Opening of the Northwest* (New York: Mariner Books, 1997), 82.

8. Bruce Hampton, *Children of Grace: The Nez Perce War of 1877* (Lincoln: University of Nebraska Press, 2002), 26.

9. Josephy, *The Nez Perce*, 217.

10. Ibid., 169.

11. Ibid., 189.

12. Spalding's autocratic treatment of the Indians was widely known at the time. Examples of his behavior can be found in Nerburn, *Chief Joseph*, 21, 32.

13. Josephy, *The Nez Perce*, 202.

14. Ibid., 205.

15. Ibid.

16. Hampton, *Children of Grace*, 27.

17. Josephy, *The Nez Perce*, 217.

18. Chief Joseph, *That All People May Be One People*, 2.

# Chapter 3

# THE STRUGGLE FOR THE LAND

## THE OREGON TERRITORY

In the aftermath of the massacre at the Whitman mission, the attention of white settlers turned to the Indians with whom they shared the territory. A fundamental misunderstanding over the land would serve as the bedrock for further hostility between the two groups. In 1845 then president James Polk abandoned the treaty that had allowed for the joint occupancy of the Oregon Territory with Great Britain. In the years prior to 1845, both nations legally occupied the territory, but neither established a government presence in the region. To have done so would have brought into question the legitimacy of the other nation's right to occupy the land.

When the treaty of joint occupancy was agreed to, the issue over which nation would possess the Oregon Territory seemed to favor the British. The United States and England had recently concluded the War of 1812, and there was only a scant American presence in the region. In contrast, England's Hudson Bay Company had occupied the land for several years. By the 1820s, all that began to change when American fur companies began to move into the area. By the end of the decade, four American companies were at work and had successfully begun to push up the Missouri River and into the territory that had once exclusively served the needs of the Hudson Bay Company.

As the American companies became more dominant in the region, the Hudson Bay Company and, by extension, the British influence began to change and eventually retreated into what is today Canada. Despite the withdrawal of the British, the issue over which nation would possess the Oregon Territory was undecided until the election of James Polk. When the treaty was dissolved, the United States claimed exclusive right to the territory, and white settlers assumed the land now belonged to them as American citizens. While the diplomatic channels between the United States and England burned with the issue of the Oregon Territory, neither nation considered it appropriate to consult with the Indians who had long resided on the land. This effectively denied the Indian people of the Columbia Plateau their claim to sovereignty and to possession of the lands they had inhabited for thousands of years. It was the mistreatment of the native people in the Oregon Territory that led to the Whitman massacre and the contest over the land.

## THE CAYUSE WAR

By early 1848, the white population in the Oregon Territory had entered into a state of war. The atrocities committed at the Waiilatpu Mission served as a precursor to further depredations throughout the territory. Because of this, all Indians were suspect, even those who were Christianized, but fear of a wider Indian war limited white transgressions against those bands. The provisional government of Oregon was called upon to respond to the threat against the settlements, and Governor George Abernathy called for a dual approach; a militia company called the Oregon Rifles would be formed under the command of Cornelius Gilliam, and a peace commission directed by Joel Palmer, Henry A. G. Lee, and Robert Newell would see whether the other tribes in the region intended to join with the Cayuse and Umatilla.

All four men charged with this ambitious task were relative newcomers to the territory. Newell had arrived in 1840, Lee in 1843, Gilliam in 1844, and Palmer in 1845. As such these men had arrived at a time when the Oregon Territory was in a period of tremendous transition. However, among the peace commissioners, two had had significant interactions with the Indians; Newell had taken a Nez Perce woman, whom he called Kitty, as his wife, and Lee had lived among the Indians when he taught at the Lapwai Mission school from 1843 to 1844. The white settlers knew that because they were vastly outnumbered by the Indians in the region, a general Indian war could devastate their settlements.

Equally, the Cayuse Indians, who had been weakened by disease and war, knew that to prevail in a contest against the Americans, they would need to rally the other Indians in the region to their cause. Subsequently, the Cayuse sent emissaries to the numerous tribes in the Oregon Territory seeking alliances, or at the very least, seeking to prevent the other tribes from allying with the settlers. The momentum of the war continued when in late February, the Cayuse burned the Saint Anne Mission and a few days later engaged in what would become known as the Battle of Sand Hollow.

The battle went badly for the Cayuse forces under the leadership of Grey Eagle, and the Cayuse were forced to withdraw from the battle after losing eight men, including Grey Eagle. While the Oregon Rifles pursued the Cayuse into eastern Oregon, the peace commission made arrangements to meet with several leaders of the Nez Perce, including Old Joseph, early the following month. Despite Spalding's concern that Old Joseph had taken part in the depredations at the Whitman mission, he also knew that the support of the Nez Perce would be necessary for a peaceful resolution to the conflict. To encourage cooperation among the Indians, Spalding sent a letter to the Nez Perce chiefs asking them to commit to a course of peace.

## Five Crows

As the skirmishes between the Cayuse and the Oregon militia continued sporadically over the next several weeks, Old Joseph would be confronted with a choice, his Christianized half-brother, Five Crows, had joined his camp in order to recover from wounds sustained at the Battle of Sand Hollow. While Five Crows had not taken part in the initial attack on the Whitman mission, he participated in the violence that spread into the surrounding communities in its aftermath. At one point, he demanded and was given one of the white captives as a wife. For the white settlers, this was further proof of Old Joseph's complicity in the growing

conflict. However, they were also unaware that Five Crows had counseled his brother that after the failure at Sand Hollow, the war could not
be won, and he encouraged him to remain neutral.

## The Lapwai Peace Conference

When word that the peace commissioners wanted to meet with the
Nez Perce chiefs reached Old Joseph, he joined about 250 other Nez
Perce Indians at a peace conference to be held at the Lapwai Mission.
As was customary for the Indians of the Columbia Plateau, diplomatic
missions were conducted with a great deal of ceremony and decorum.
While the chiefs would be the focus of the white commissioners, their
participation in the meeting would be observed by their people where
the effectiveness of their oratory skills would be judged. Undoubtedly,
among those present was a young boy who was almost eight years old,
Young Joseph.

*Young Joseph's Role at the Conference.* While it is likely Young
Joseph, like his siblings and mother, accompanied his father to the peace
council, he would have maintained a respectful distance from his father. Among the Nez Perce, open affection between parents and their
children was not common; this, however, did not mean that parents and
children had little regard or interaction with each other. Instead, within
the Nez Perce culture, children were expected to watch and mimic their
parents. Young Joseph, who had been marked to be a leader among his
people from the moment of his birth, would have been expected to re-
spectfully watch his father at the peace council, but not to interfere.

Many of the basic skills Young Joseph would learn in his life would
be taught to him by close relatives or friends of his parents; however,
the skills of diplomacy that would characterize his service to his people
would be taught through the example of his father and the other headmen of the tribe. In this way, a child was able to observe several similar
ways of achieving the same thing, which gave him greater flexibility in
determining how he would perform the same tasks when the responsibility fell on his shoulders. Young Joseph would then be expected to take
the skills he had observed in his father at the council and mitigate issues
among his contemporaries. At the Lapwai peace council, Young Joseph

would have seen his father's ardent desire for peace and his respect for the Christian religion.

**Negotiations with the Peace Commissioners.**    At the meeting, Old Joseph addressed the commissioners and asserted his desire for peace with the white settlers and of his commitment to Christianity and the missions. Old Joseph insisted he would not join with those who had murdered the settlers at the Whitman mission. Old Joseph's eloquent speech was followed by similar speeches from Timothy, James, and several others. Palmer listened intently to the speeches, and when they had finished, he advised the Indians of the American position regarding the massacre.

Palmer insisted the Cayuse had forfeited their lands when they attacked the mission and encouraged the Nez Perce to try to convince the Cayuse to surrender those guilty of the attack. Palmer then ordered the Nez Perce to return to their lands and to resume the farming and peaceful activities they had engaged in before the massacre. He promised he would prevent other settlers from coming onto their lands so long as they lived in peace. The Nez Perce readily agreed to Palmer's proposal and tried to convince the Cayuse to surrender the murderers of the Whitmans, but when they were unsuccessful in their entreaties, they returned to their lands.

## The Oregon Rifles

By May the Cayuse warriors were still on the warpath, and the Oregon Rifles, now led by Henry A. G. Lee, doggedly continued in their pursuit. Frustrated by their lack of success, Lee offered the Nez Perce several hundred dollars' worth of merchandise if they would assist in the capture of the renegade Indians. Lee's offer was not without its merits. Since the outbreak of the war, Indians had been prevented from purchasing gunpowder and guns. This effectively meant the Indians were unable to defend themselves and, in many instances, were unable to continue to hunt to support their families. Additionally, with the outbreak of hostilities, the regular subsistence patterns of the Nez Perce and the other tribes in the region were interrupted, and subsequently, they were unable to gather the food they needed for the winter ahead. Because of this, hunting increased in its importance to the tribe.

### The End of the War

The Cayuse War continued sporadically for the next seven years. The Cayuse refused to surrender to the Oregon forces and continued to alternately strike at the white settlements and then retreat into the relative sanctuary of the Blue Mountains. As the months stretched into years, those who participated in the conflict changed. Colonel Gilliam was killed accidently in 1848, and pursuit of the Cayuse fell to the U.S. Army.

## THE OREGON DONATION ACT AND THE INDIAN TREATY ACT

By 1850 the tide was turning against the Indians of the Columbia Plateau. In that year, the new state of Oregon passed the Oregon Donation Land Act, which allowed any white, male resident of the state to claim 320 acres of land from the public domain, and if the man were married, his wife could claim another 320 acres. The only problem with the Donation Act was that there was no public domain. The land belonged to the Indian tribes. To rectify this, Congress followed the Donation Act with the Indian Treaty Act.

The Indian Treaty Act authorized commissioners to purchase land from the Indians, establish reservations for them, and then remove those Indians to the newly agreed upon reservations. The largest problem with this plan was that settlers did not wait for the commissioners to complete their work and often moved onto lands that were still held by the tribes. Legitimately or not, this land giveaway drew still more people into the plateau and further challenged the ability of the Cayuse and the other tribes to remain aloof from the white population.

Eventually, Congress would order the commissioners to suspend all further treaty negotiations and refused to ratify the ones that had been agreed to because those treaties favored the tribes over the white settlers. By the middle of the year, the Cayuse, tired of war and of being fugitives in a land they once called their own, agreed to surrender the five men the government had demanded early in the conflict.

## THE SURRENDER OF THE CAYUSE

In May 1850, five Cayuse warriors, *Tilokaikt, Tomahas, Klokamas, Isaiachalkis,* and *Kimasumpkin* surrendered to U.S. Marshal Joseph Meek.

Shortly after their surrender, they were tried and convicted of murder by a military commission. All five were hung on June 3 of that same year.

The execution of the five Cayuse leaders did not end the war, nor for many did it represent justice; *Kimasumpkin* long denied his involvement in the massacre, and there is little proof to counter his contention. Perhaps this is why the violence did not end with the executions. Instead, another five bloody years of conflict lay in the future. During the Cayuse War, one individual appears only sporadically in the records of the missions and the settlements of the Oregon Territory, Old Joseph. Disgusted with the violence and the behavior of those on both sides of the war, and unwilling to involve his people in the conflict, Old Joseph and his people moved out of harm's way and back into the mountain passes of the Wallowa Valley.

## OLD JOSEPH'S RETREAT TO THE WALLOWA VALLEY

Old Joseph's decision to remove his people from the influence of the settlers and the missionaries would serve as an unmistakable criticism of how the missions had conducted themselves over the previous years. The central ideas of Christianity were peace and harmony, yet little peace or harmony had prevailed in the Columbia Plateau since their arrival. Old Joseph noted that those who most often spoke of justice were the first to take up arms, and that the missionaries were often complicit in the hostilities that seemed to continue unabated. Old Joseph's rationale for moving his people may also have been more practical in nature.

By the early 1850s, only 3,000 Nez Perce lived in the Columbia Plateau, and they were not united as they had once been. Those who had adopted Christianity now accounted for roughly 60 percent of the tribe, and they often took the side of the settlers over their kinsmen, which effectively reduced the overall strength of the Nez Perce people. While Old Joseph's abandonment of the Lapwai Mission was a slap against the practices of missionary Henry Spalding and the others, it did not mean their efforts had been a complete failure.

When the missionary board decided that the conflicts in the territory were no longer worth the risk of keeping the mission open, several prominent chiefs—namely, Lawyer, Red Wolf, and Timothy—remained loyal to Christianity and what they had learned from Spalding and his wife. As they gained prominence in the region, they encouraged their people to become farmers and to embrace the ways of the white man. Additionally, the Spaldings did not leave the Oregon country, instead they moved into the Willamette Valley and helped to establish a school there while Henry assumed a position as a pastor of a local congregation. Eliza Spalding died in 1851, but Henry would continue to be involved with the Nez Perce for several more years to come. With more settlers coming into the region and several powerful Nez Perce bands adopting Christianity, the permanence of both was assured in the region. However, this also ensured that conflict would become a permanent fixture in the region.

## THE APPOINTMENT OF ISAAC STEVENS

As white settlers continued to pour into the Oregon Territory, formalized agreements with the tribes were needed. Because of the vast size of the Oregon Territory, which included modern-day Oregon and Washington and parts of Idaho and Montana, it was divided into smaller parcels that approximate those current states boundaries. In 1853 then president Franklin Pierce appointed a hero of the Mexican-American War and ardent political supporter Isaac Stevens as governor and superintendent of Indian Affairs in the newly created Washington Territory.

Stevens had been given a mandate to secure Indian land for the United States. Unfortunately, his tactics reveal a man who was at the same time intractable, deceitful, and aggressive. His appointment as governor and superintendent was not sufficient for Stevens, who was a man with lofty ambitions. Before leaving Washington, D.C., to assume his post, Stevens actively campaigned for and received a third appointment as a railroad surveyor for the Pacific Northwest. Since transportation corridors like the railroad represented economic growth for a region, the individuals who surveyed the land and chose the routes for the railroads were in an enviable position to make money. The only hindrance to Stevens's goals of increasing the public domain and advancing American possession of the territory were the Indians. To Stevens the solution was simple: they would need to be bent to his will.

# THE WALLA WALLA TREATY CONFERENCE

Reminiscent of the tactics attempted by Elijah White a decade earlier, Stevens abandoned negotiation and instead merely sought to impose his will upon the native people of the Northwest. Once he had finished his task in the Washington Territory, Stevens moved south and by May 1855 held a treaty conference with the Nez Perce and other tribes at Mill Creek in the Walla Walla Valley. At this treaty council, an estimated 5,000 Indians attended, including Old Joseph, who spoke for his people, and Young Joseph, who by now had entered his teens and was keenly observing his father's actions.

While Stevens was intractable and aggressive, his actions were tempered by those of Joel Palmer, the former peace commissioner, who translated for Stevens and often softened his abrasive tone in order to keep the negotiations on a friendly keel. Despite Stevens's desire to originally create one large reservation for all the Indians of the region, divisions within the tribes forced the concession that three reserves would be established. One would serve the Nez Perce; another, the Umatilla, Cayuse, and Walla Walla; and the last, the Yakima Indians and other small bands. While Stevens had envisioned a brief encounter with unsophisticated Indians who could be easily manipulated to his will, what he encountered were tribal representatives who responded to his demands with intelligence and diplomacy.

## Lawyer and the Christianized Indians

In seeking to obtain consensus among themselves and the Americans, the representatives of the various bands of Indians at the council prolonged the proceedings for two weeks. The principal negotiator for the Nez Perce was *Hallalhotsoot*, or "Lawyer," the son of Twisted Hair, the chief who had met Lewis and Clark a half century earlier. As a Christian, Lawyer did not fully represent the interests of all the Nez Perce, because those who had wholly accepted Christianity attempted to live in accordance with white traditions, such as farming and ranching, all of which required significantly less land than that required by their traditional brethren. Complaints that Lawyer was too easily swayed by Stevens and the U.S. representatives clouded the council. However, at the end

of two weeks, an agreement had been reached; the Nez Perce agreed
to cede approximately 40 percent of their land to the U.S. government
in exchange for peace and other concessions.

## Impact of Looking Glass at the Treaty Conference

However, before the treaty was signed, Chief *Allalimya Takanin,* or
"Looking Glass," of the Nez Perce arrived at the council. Looking Glass
had been away on a buffalo hunt when the negotiations began, and arrived only to find that the discussions had ended. Undaunted, Looking
Glass quickly involved himself in the proceedings, and when he found
out what Lawyer had agreed to was reported to have said, "My people
what have you done? While I was gone, you have sold my country."[1]

Looking Glass attempted to redesign the boundaries of Nez Perce territory, but the die had been cast, and the treaty was signed by 57 Nez
Perce leaders, including Old Joseph. The impact of this treaty probably
had a great influence on the teenaged Young Joseph. Over a period of
several weeks, he had witnessed how desperately his father wanted to
maintain peace with the white community, even to the point of con-
ceding lands that had been part of Nez Perce territory for countless generations.

## The Failure of the Walla Walla Treaty

Under the Walla Walla Treaty, the Nez Perce were limited to a reserve
of 8 million acres from their previous bounty of 14 million. In exchange
for the land, they were guaranteed to live in perpetual peace with the
white settlers and would receive yearly annuities to make up for the
loss of their land. However, despite the promises of the commissioners,
the provisions of the treaty were ignored almost immediately. The goods
promised to the Nez Perce would take six years to arrive, and by then, the
people of the Columbia Plateau had a larger issue to contend with—gold.

# THE DISCOVERY OF GOLD
# ALONG THE CLEARWATER

By 1851 gold had been found on the Nez Perce reservation in the Rogue
and Umpqua rivers of Oregon, and later throughout what would become Washington State. The find resulted in a flood of miners who

crowded with Nez Perce and led to the seemingly inevitable violence as the two groups struggled for control of the region's limited resources. By 1860 miners hit the mother lode along the Clearwater watershed, and still more whites flooded into the region. The provisions of the treaty seemed to be all but forgotten by the white population.

The territorial and federal governments demonstrated little inclination toward halting the establishment and growth of white settlements in Nez Perce land. However, control of the Indians was a different matter; in 1861 the federal government assigned an Indian agent to a newly established Nez Perce Agency in an attempt to reduce the tension between the miners and the Nez Perce. However, this peaceful gesture was offset by the assignment of two companies of soldiers to the newly formed Fort Lapwai which was constructed on the Lapwai Reservation. The desire of the government to maintain peaceful relations with the Nez Perce came into question the following year when Henry Spalding returned to Lapwai.

## THE RETURN OF HENRY SPALDING

Spalding was well received by the Nez Perce whom he had not seen since the Whitman massacre in 1847; however, his attempts to interact with the Nez Perce were repeatedly blocked by the new Indian agent and made the successful completion of his missionary duties all but impossible. Because he was seen as a conflicting source of authority for the Indians, Spalding's authority was marginalized by the agent. With an internal conflict festering again between the white men who had been called to serve the Nez Perce people, the new agency and its agent were subsequently rendered ineffective in resolving any serious issues that erupted between the miners and the Indians.

Many of the now 18,000 whites who lived in the region held little in common with the missionaries who had arrived in the area a generation before. To many of these new settlers, the Indians were not entitled to the land; it had been fairly won in a contest between Great Britain and America, and as citizens of the United States, they had a right to enjoy the rewards of that contest. For these men, the Indians were little more than a hindrance to their prosperity, and lawless behavior directed against the Indians became increasingly more commonplace. To avoid provoking an all-out Indian war, a new treaty was needed. Unfortunately, it would be one that would accommodate the new settlers at the expense of the Nez Perce.

## THE THIEF TREATY

By 1863 the issue reached crisis proportions, and the federal government searched for a way to remedy the situation. The U.S. government finally decided that remedy would be the renegotiation of the 1855 treaty and the concession of more land. For the Nez Perce and the other Indians who had been part of the 1855 treaty, the government's position made little sense. The government, in failing to meet its obligations, now sought another treaty of concession in order to protect its interests.

Oregon Superintendent of Indian Affairs Calvin Hale called for a treaty council to be held at Lapwai in May 1863. Hale retained Henry Spalding and Robert Newell as interpreters for the government, and Lawyer again appeared as the chief negotiator for the Nez Perce. However, Lawyer's role in this second treaty would be more controversial than his role at the treaty negotiations in 1855.

Disgusted at the demand for renegotiation a mere eight years after the original agreement had been signed, several Nez Perce chiefs refused to attend the treaty council; others walked away from the negotiations when it became clear that the government had no intention of enforcing the provisions of the 1855 treaty and instead merely sought a greater concession of land. Subsequently, most of the Indians present at this treaty council were from Lawyer's band. However, Old Joseph attended and brought with him Young Joseph to observe the proceedings. When Hale indicated the government's position was to obtain additional land concessions, Lawyer reminded him that the provisions of the previous treaty had not been met and that most of the prominent chiefs of the Nez Perce were absent. Hale brushed off this inconvenient fact and continued to insist on the land cession.

Lawyer himself, as recorded in the official minutes from the negotiations, gave no indication that he spoke for the other Nez Perce bands. However, his willingness to negotiate, and his previous service during the 1855 treaty negotiations, settled him in the minds of the white representatives as the voice of the Nez Perce people. The federal government insisted that Lawyer spoke on behalf of all the Nez Perce people, and no one rose to vocally counter this argument. By June several additional chiefs had arrived at Lapwai and by consensus agreed to sell land that had already been occupied by whites and where gold had been found, but nothing else. Hale did not hide his disappointment in this proposal; he had been sent to negotiate land concessions, not purchase, and flatly refused the proposal.

Because the government was no longer negotiating and instead had devolved into attempting to dictate terms, most of the chiefs left the council or refused to participate further. Of those who remained, few were more than subchiefs, and under the influence of Lawyer, most had been Christianized, and none would be impacted by the further loss of land. By the time the negotiations were completed, 52 Nez Perce Indians, of whom the most prominent was Lawyer, signed a treaty that ceded more than 90 percent of the 8 million acres that had been part of the Nez Perce reserve. Concessions to allow off-reservation fishing and hunting were retained from the previous 1855 treaty, but essentially the land of the Nez Perce would be taken from them, and they would be expected to reside on the newly created Lapwai Reservation.

## Lawyer's Treaty Concessions

Because the Civil War was preoccupying the attention of America in 1863, the treaty would not be ratified by Congress until 1867. Lawyer's actions have been fraught with controversy since he placed his signature on the treaty in 1863. Lawyer's actions went against Nez Perce tradition, which held that no man could speak for another, nor could he give away or sell land that was not held by his own band. Often, those defending Lawyer will point out that he did not indicate he was speaking for all the bands of Nez Perce. However, this argument neglects to address the fundamental truth that Lawyer signed a treaty that conceded the disposal of lands that were not his to give and that were occupied by most of the non-Christianized Nez Perce. As such, Lawyer's actions must be viewed in another light.

With a sharply reduced land base, Lawyer's agreement would have forced the traditional Nez Perce to accept American-style farming in order to be able to sustain themselves. This might also make the Nez

Perce more prone to accept Christianity, something that would have appealed to Lawyer as this would have increased his authority over the Nez Perce. At the time of the signing of what became known as the Thief Treaty, less than 50 percent of the Nez Perce had accepted Christianity and were living in accordance with white civilization; the remaining members of the tribe, including the band led by Old Joseph, had held fast to their traditional subsistence patterns. Old Joseph, like the other traditional bands of Nez Perce, reasoned that since he and his people already had agreed to the 1855 Walla Walla Treaty, no further negotiations would be necessary.

## Chief Joseph's Participation at the Treaty Conference

However, since any treaty negotiation would impact his people, Old Joseph who was now "blind and feeble,"[2] charged his son to serve as his proxy during the proceedings and to speak for the band. Young Joseph, now 23, assumed the mantle of tribal chief and during the council proceedings clearly stated his band's position to the white men present. Young Joseph insisted that "the white man had no right to take our country. We have never accepted presents from the government. Neither Lawyer nor any other chief has authority to sell this land. It has always belonged to my people."[3] Young Joseph's insistence, however, had little effect on the overall proceedings.

When Old Joseph was informed of the treaty, he was disgusted at the duplicity of the white settlers. According to Joseph, his "father was the first to see through the schemes of the white men, and he warned his tribe to be careful about trading with them. He had a suspicion of men who seemed so anxious to make money . . . He had sharper eyes than the rest of our people."[4] Despite his cautionary advice, Old Joseph was powerless to stop Lawyer from signing the 1863 treaty, but it would serve as the final break between his band and the whites who had come to his land.

## Old Joseph's Rejection of Christianity

When the missionaries came to teach the Nez Perce about the "Book of Heaven" and Christianity, they had insisted that this was the religion of the white man, that Christianity served as the core of white culture, and that truth, peace, and justice were reflections of Christianity's influence. When confronted with the realization that the "white men were growing rich very fast and were greedy to possess everything the Indian had,"[5] Old Joseph came to the conclusion that the religion of the white man was little more than a ruse. He reportedly tore up his Bible after the 1863 treaty council and returned to the traditional religion of his forefathers.

### Lawyer's Private Negotiations

While the whites in the region considered the treaty to be law, they still readily ignored many of the provisions to which they had agreed. This failure eventually drew the ire of Lawyer himself who found a solution. In 1868 Lawyer and three other Nez Perce chiefs traveled to Washington, D.C., in an attempt to compel the government to honor its treaty agreement. As Lawyer would later complain, "If [Stevens] had told us that the reservation was to be flooded with white settlers, or that the saw mill was to be used for the exclusive benefit of the Whites, we would never have consented to the treaty."[6]

Lawyer's efforts eventually bore fruit when a supplement to the 1863 treaty was agreed to. In this supplement, which is often known as the Treaty of 1868, the most desirable land on the Lapwai Reservation would be surveyed and then distributed by the agent or the Nez Perce chiefs to the Indians within their bands. Additionally, a provision was made to allow Indians not living on the reservation to retain up to 20 acres of land if they had made improvements on the land. This last provision would have excluded the traditional Indians like Joseph and his band since the improvements that would have been considered would have been fences, homesteads, or other permanent structures. Effectively, Lawyer had settled on a way to divide the land of his forefathers into individual parcels that would reflect the changing lifestyle of the Christianized Indians, and that would dispossess the nontreaty Indians of their lands.

## GRANT'S PEACE POLICY

Lawyer's actions on behalf of the Christianized Indians meshed with a change in federal Indian policy, under the nation's new president, Ulysses Grant. Under what became known as Grant's Peace Policy, all Indians would be confined to reserves. Here they would be isolated from the white settlements and would learn to be civilized. Once this had been achieved, the Indians would be ready to assume their place in white society. This civilizing process would be overseen by Indian agents who were most often members of large religious organizations. Those Indians who refused to confine themselves to the reservations would be considered belligerent and thus could fall under the control of the army, which would deal with the tribes by force. The chief proponents for Grant's policy were the missionary groups that saw the opportunity to minister to and convert the Indians, while those opposed were primarily members of the military upon whose shoulders rested the mandate to protect settlers in the far flung reaches of the nation. To the military, the Indians should not be tutored in the ways of civilized life; instead, it should be dictated to them.

## OLD JOSEPH'S DESPERATE ATTEMPT TO RETAIN HIS LANDS

Lawyer's acceptance of the 1863 Thief Treaty signaled the influx of still greater numbers of white settlers into the Columbia Plateau. Much of this influx slowed when the gold reserves began to slow in the early years of the 1860s and when the Civil War in the East drew men away from the Pacific Northwest, but enough still continued to arrive in the land of the Nez Perce that competition for the resources in the region would eventually become acute. After the Thief Treaty had been signed, Joseph reported that an agent came to their people and insisted that the "Great White Chief at Washington"[7] wanted his band to move to the newly created Lapwai Reservation. The band refused, and because the issues that had originally driven the treaty were abating, the issue was not pressed.

Old Joseph, well aware that the desire of the white man was to take the land of his forefathers and certain that he would never agree to such a concession took to erecting piles of stones and poles at the edges of the land claimed by the Wal-lam-wat-kin band to identify that this was their land, a trick he had learned from observing the land surveyors who had been sent by the government. According to Chief Joseph, his father told him, "Inside is the home of my people—the white man may take

Chief Joseph (In-mut-too-yah-lat-lat) of the Nez Perce. It was his quiet leadership that enabled many within the Nez Perce tribe to survive the trials that confronted them in 1877. While many white Americans attributed the military genius displayed by the Nez Perce to Joseph, he had been against war and their infamous flight. Photographed by William H. Jackson, before 1877. American Indian Select List number 102. Courtesy National Archives, ARC ID # 523670.

the land outside. Inside this boundary all our people were born. It circles the graves of our fathers, and we will never give up these graves to any man."[8] Old Joseph was also aware that the time he had left to protect his people was fading. Born around the year 1785, Old Joseph was in his late seventies or early eighties at the time the Thief Treaty was signed. His strength was fading quickly, although his mind remained alert. As the decade stretched on, he passed more of the responsibility for the daily management of the tribe to his son. He instructed Joseph not to agree to sell the lands of their ancestors and to refuse to accept any gift from a white man so he would never be accused of having sold the land.

## JOSEPH'S FIRST MARRIAGE AND CHILD

During the seeming interlude of peace when the numbers of white settlers declined, Joseph took his first wife, *Heyoon yoyikt*, the daughter of another Nez Perce chief named *Whisk-tasket*. By 1865, Joseph and Heyoon yoyikt welcomed their first child into the world; they would name her

*Heyoon yoyikt, ca. 1880. She was the first of Chief Joseph's five wives. She accompanied him through the flight of the Nez Perce in 1877 and into captivity. Reproduction number NA 626. Courtesy University of Washington.*

*Hophoponmi*, or "Noise of Running Feet." Protected in the isolated mountain passes of the Wallowa Valley, Joseph entered this mature stage of his life with a foot planted firmly in both worlds. At times the isolation of their mountain retreat would have encouraged many to think that the white man was far away and their homeland was protected. At other times, however, when forced to leave their retreat for trade or to gather the food needed for the winter, the number of houses that dotted a landscape that previously had been void of human settlement would have reminded them that their peace would be short lived.

When the Civil War in the East concluded in early 1865, the pent up energy of a nation seemed to be released into the West. Crews of men gathered to build the transcontinental railroad, and the promise of free land through the Homestead Act attracted thousands into the once pristine landscape. As conflicts between these new settlers and the traditional Indians increased, the groups of Indians who refused to move onto reservations began to band together out of necessity and shared interests. With their traditional way of life under attack, these tribes experienced an upsurge in the Washani religion. For Joseph it seemed the white man was interested in land alone and would do anything in order to get what he wanted.

## JOSEPH AS THE POLITICAL LEADER OF HIS PEOPLE

For Joseph, his ring side seat at the treaty negotiations and their impact on his tribe must have weighed heavily on him, for unlike most Nez Perce men, Young Joseph had been chosen for a path that required him to remain at the center of the maelstrom that consumed both the whites and his people in order to better understand what was happening and from there to better serve his band. As a diplomatic leader of his people, Young Joseph's place was with his people, not in the quiet mountains of his ancestral home. In this way, he would be more acutely aware of what was happening and could respond more effectively in order to ensure their safety. Because of this, instead of taking to the plains to hunt for the buffalo or the large game animals as his brother Ollokot would have, he remained at home.

### Death of Old Joseph

Without complaint, Joseph embraced his role as a diplomat for his people. By the beginning of the 1870s, Old Joseph's health had continued its downward spiral, and while he offered advice to his son, he had long since abdicated the responsibility for the well-being of the band to his son. However, as Old Joseph began to feel his life ebbing, he called Joseph to him and gave him the last of his sage advice: "You are the chief of these people. They look to you to guide them. Always remember that your father never sold his country. You must stop your ears when you are asked to sign a treaty selling your home. A few years more and white men will be all around you. They have their eyes on this land. My son, never forget my dying words. This country holds your father's body.

Never sell the bones of your father and your mother.'"[9] Joseph promised to protect the land and the graves of his parents, and thus reassured, his father died.

Old Joseph was buried at the base of a hill along the Wallowa and Lostine rivers in the lower part of the Wallowa Valley. A barrier was erected around his grave, and from a crosspole was strung a bell that would chime when pushed by the wind. To the followers of the Dreamer religion, the ringing of a bell signified moments of great importance. Sadly, the body of Old Joseph would not be allowed to rest undisturbed. In 1886 his grave was opened and scavengers stole the skull of the old chief and placed it on display in a dentist's office; eventually, the skull was lost. Old Joseph's death in August 1871 would signal the last moments of peace in the Wallowa Valley, by the end of the winter in 1872, conditions had begun spiraling out of control and challenged the promises Chief Joseph had made to his father.

## Reopening of the Lapwai Mission

As Old Joseph was preparing for this death in the summer of 1871, Henry Spalding reentered the world of the Nez Perce. Despite the tragedy of the Whitman Massacre almost a quarter of a century earlier, Spalding had not forgotten his desire to lead the Nez Perce into Christianity. However, the closure of the Lapwai Mission in 1848 had prevented him from continuing his ministration to them. However, with the advent of President Ulysses Grant's Peace Policy, he was assigned to reopen the Lapwai Mission and resume his duties of converting and civilizing the Indians. With many of the Nez Perce already willing converts to Christianity, he enjoyed considerably more success than what he had experienced when he first arrived in 1836.

However, Spalding was unable to convince Joseph to return to the fold of the church. As the leader of his people, Joseph had witnessed both the light and dark side of the white settlers who had entered into the land of his people. He understood that in a war, the Nez Perce would not win because they were not united as a people and because the numbers against them would have been too great. But he hoped that his band's home in the isolated retreats of the mountainous Imnaha Valley would be enough to protect them; sadly, this would not prove to be the case.

When completed in 1869, the transcontinental railroad brought a steady stream of settlers into his land. When confronted by this challenge, Joseph sought to respond in a peaceful and measured way to the issues that threatened his people. Instead of violence, he attempted on several occasions to explain to Spalding and the new representative of the government, the Indian agent John Monteith, that his people did not want to live as the white man did and why they rejected the Thief Treaty. Whenever Monteith insisted on the validity of the treaty, Joseph calmly reminded him that his people had never agreed to further land concessions and that his father's signature was not on the treaty.

Joseph also gently rebuffed Henry Spalding's attempts to entice Joseph and his band to return to the Lapwai Mission. While Joseph had been baptized by Spalding shortly after his birth, he had largely been raised within the traditional beliefs of his people and saw no reason to embrace Christianity. However, his understanding of the beliefs that underscored Christianity prompted him to believe that America would remain faithful to her beliefs and to the promises made to the Nez Perce people. Despite his reasoned arguments time would prove that the religious beliefs of the settlers did not extend to the issue of native land.

## WHITE SETTLEMENT IN THE WALLOWA VALLEY

As the winter of 1871–1872 approached, the band left the high country of the Wallowa Mountains for their winter retreat in the Imnaha Valley along the Snake River. The summer of 1871 had been a dry one for the region surrounding the Wallowa Valley, and subsequently, the once plentiful hay crops withered in the blistering heat. The specter of starving livestock and lost profits loomed over the farms of the white settlers who had settled in the region. The Wallowa Valley alone seemed immune to the devastation of the drought that year, and subsequently, white settlers began to move into the valley, just as the Nez Perce moved into the protected Imnaha Valley for the winter.

When the band returned to their summer camps the following year, whites had already built cabins along the waterways and were pasturing their herds in the fields. Their actions denied the Nez Perce access to their lands and their herds access to the grass upon which they were dependent. Joseph confronted the trespassers and asked them to leave, but the settlers insisted that the 1863 Thief Treaty gave them the right to remain. Unable to sway the settlers, Joseph appealed to the Indian agent, Monteith, to intercede for them, but he too had little success in compelling the settlers to leave.

## Forced Concessions in the Wallowa Valley

In August 1872, Monteith brokered a meeting between the Indians and the white settlers to discuss their occupation of the land. However, once the settlers were aware that Joseph did not intend to fight, they refused his request to leave, and eventually the two sides settled into an impasse. Monteith addressed the issue in his report to Francis Amasa Walker, the commissioner of Indian Affairs and encouraged the commissioner to consider "if there was any way in which the Wallowa Valley could be kept for the Indians, I would recommend that it be done."[10] However, Joseph knew that the government would not support the Nez Perce in their claim to the land, and that there was little short of war that he could do to compel the whites to leave his ancestral home.

As Joseph would later note, "Through all the years since the white man came to Wallowa, we have been threatened and taunted by them and the treaty Nez Perces. They have given us no rest . . . I have carried a heavy load on my back since I was a boy. I learned then that we were but few, while the white men were many, and that we could not hold our own with them."[11] Eventually, the Nez Perce agreed that the settlers could stay, so long as no more came. The agreement between the settlers and the Nez Perce was broken almost as soon as it had been agreed to, and more white settlers appeared in the valley.

## The Discovery of Gold in the Wallowa Valley

By 1873 the conflict over land threatened to explode into a wider conflict when gold was found in the mountains surrounding the Wallowa Valley and more settlers and miners moved into the region. These individuals had no intention of building communities or living in peace with the Indians. They had come to get rich and then to move on to greener pastures, and they demonstrated no respect for the possessions of the Indians. As Joseph reported, "They stole many horses from us . . . The white men told lies for each other. They drove off a great many of our cattle. Some white men branded our young cattle so they could claim them. We had no friend who would plead our cause before the law councils . . . They knew we were not strong enough to fight them."[12] By 1873 the issue of the nontreaty Indians was one that could no longer be ignored. Soon resentment on the part of the Indians or on the part of the white settlers would have erupted into war. Despite the disturbing trend that confronted the Nez Perce Indians over the control of their land, it would be another tribe farther to the west that would first draw the attention of the nation.

## The Modoc War

As conditions in the Wallowa Valley deteriorated, the people of the United States were reminded that the Indians, while declining in numbers, were still a force to be contended with. In the late 1860s, conditions for the Modoc Indians in northern California seemed to mirror what was happening to the Nez Perce in the northern territories. The Modoc had been compelled to sign a treaty ceding most of their land and had agreed to move onto the Klamath Reservation in order to make room for more white settlement. However, the Klamath Reservation was already crowded with other tribes from the region, including the traditional enemies of the Modoc, the Klamath Indians. When the two groups were forced into close proximity, the Klamath began to harass the Modoc and rather than stay and endure the abuse, a small band quit the reservation and returned to their traditional lands.

Led by *Kintpuash*, or "Captain Jack," the Modoc were chased by the federal government in an attempt to return them to the overcrowded reservation. When the Indians refused to return, the situation devolved into what became known as the Modoc War. In this brief but riveting war, which lasted from 1872 to 1873, some 57 white soldiers were killed, including their commander, Edward Canby, and another 46 were wounded. The Modoc lost 13 warriors and were forced to return to the reservation. Several of their leaders, including Captain Jack, were tried, convicted, and hung for their part in the war. The band of Modoc that held off the U.S. Army never numbered more than 60 men and women while the forces against them were more than 10 times greater than that. The lesson of the Modoc War was not lost on whites in the region. With his band numbering in the hundreds, Joseph could prove to be a considerable threat to the white settlements if sufficiently provoked. For that reason, some concession on the part of the government was needed.

## The Division of the Valley

In his annual report to the commissioner of Indian Affairs in Washington, agent John Monteith reported that the valley was "so high and cold that they can raise nothing but the hardiest of vegetables . . . The valley is surrounded by high mountains and it is impossible to get a wagon in the valley until a road is built."[13] Economic development would take considerable effort and investment, something that was unlikely considering the limited potential for a sufficient economic return. Unwilling to eject the settlers from the Wallowa Valley, the new commissioner of Indian Affairs, Edward P. Smith, directed Monteith and T. B. Odneal, the superintendent of Indian Affairs in Oregon, to find an acceptable solution to the dilemma. Since the Indians refused to leave the Wallowa Valley and settle on the Lapwai Reservation, the government proposed the division of the Wallowa Valley.

Since most of the white settlement had begun in the lower part of the Wallowa Valley, Monteith and Odneal recommended that this be set aside for whites, while the upper valley where the Nez Perce primarily lived would be reserved for their use. To secure the Indians' agreement on this in March 1873, Monteith called for a council at Lapwai. At the council, Joseph reiterated his position that the valley had never been ceded to the government and of the invalidity of the 1863 treaty. In their report to the Indian commissioner following the council, Monteith and Odneal agreed that the validity of the 1863 treaty was central to the dispute and that prudence dictated that the legitimacy of the treaty be ascertained before proceeding with a division of the land. If the treaty was found to be invalid, the government should move the settlers off the land and provide compensation for any improvements they had made. However, if the treaty was valid, the division of the land could proceed without delay.

Despite the concerns over the validity of the Thief Treaty, Joseph knew there were few options available to him; the government had widely ignored its treaties in the past, and there was little support for the idea that they would remove the settlers if they found the treaty to be invalid. As such, Joseph tentatively agreed to the provisions of the council that called for the division of the valley. However, Secretary of the Interior Columbus Delano, who oversaw Indian affairs, chose to ignore the issue of the validity of the 1863 treaty and recommended instead that the upper Wallowa Valley be designated by executive order as an Indian reserve, not through treaty, which would have given the Indians greater legal claim to the land.

## Error in Grant's Executive Order

On June 16, 1873, President Ulysses Grant approved the designation and ordered part of the Wallowa Valley to become the Nez Perce reservation. However, while the Indians, settlers, and the agents all agreed that the Nez Perce should have the upper valley, the executive order

*President Ulysses S. Grant's executive order created a reservation in the Wallowa Valley for Joseph and his people. Confusion would eventually force the retraction of the order. Library of Congress.*

signed by Grant reversed the land grant; the settlers were given the upper valley, and the Nez Perce were assigned to the lower valley. This simple clerical error should have been immediately corrected, and the agreement completed as discussed. However, instead of correcting the mistake, the government became paralyzed by inaction, and this allowed conditions to spiral out of control.

When the Nez Perce returned to the Wallowa Valley in the spring of 1873, the division of the land had not been formalized and during the previous winter more settlers had entered into the valley. Young Nez Perce warriors became engaged in fights with these settlers over live-stock and grazing privileges. While the elders in the tribes counseled patience and peace, the response from the settlers ensured that would not occur. A flurry of rumors began to sweep through the valley that the Indians were planning a war. To protect themselves the settlers formed a militia unit and erected a stockade.

## RUMORS OF WAR IN THE WALLOWA VALLEY

As one settler commented in the *Mountain Sentinel* newspaper in May of that year, "We only propose protection to ourselves against depredations of unfriendly Indians."[14] While the white inhabitants of the Wallowa Valley were preparing for war, the Nez Perce moved to the northern part of the valley, into land that was designated as theirs under the proposed executive order reservation, in order to reduce contact between them-selves and the settlers. This, however, did not quiet the maelstrom of complaints that plagued the valley. White business investors, who did not live in the valley and who had taken no part in the agreement, joined the fray and complained that a reservation in the Wallowa Valley would hinder the development of roads and trade through the region. Mount-ing criticism over the agreement that was directed at the federal govern-ment only seemed to add to the morass.

### Demise of the Wallowa Reservation

Agent Monteith, well aware of his central position in the conflict mael-strom, tried to pressure Joseph and his band to settle down and begin farming in the valley. Joseph refused and insisted his people would live in accordance with their traditional ways. In frustration, Monteith recommended in his annual report at the end of the year that he was "of the opinion that Joseph and his band are not entitled to the Wallowa unless they go there and settle down."[15] Relations between Monteith and the other nontreaty Indians deteriorated further when he attempted to force the Indians to remain at the Lapwai Reservation. Without the support of the agent who had been charged to represent their interests, and with the rising crescendo of complaints against the executive order that had created the Wallowa Valley reserve, the federal government began to back away from its position.

In 1874 Commissioner Smith wrote that "nothing more would be done toward establishing a reservation"[16] in the valley. The government ceased any activity that would have led to a formal survey of the Wallowa Valley and the establishment of the boundaries of the proposed reserve. All discussion of removing the white settlers and of providing compensation to them ceased, but the federal government refused to inform the Indians of the change in federal policy. Instead, authorities hunkered down to see what would happen next. With each side now locked into a different understanding of their rights, relations between the settlers and the Nez Perce became increasingly more hostile. The region was poised to explode into violence; all that was needed were a few sparks to ignite a war.

Away from the prying eyes of the residents of the Wallowa Valley, the governor of Oregon also weighed in on the controversy surrounding the valley. Governor LaFayette F. Grover began writing a series of letters to the secretary of the interior encouraging him to rescind the 1873 executive order. Grover insisted that the Wallowa Valley was already settled by "enterprising white families" and that if the land were allowed to revert back to its "aboriginal character . . . a very serious check will be given to the growth of our frontier settlements."[17] Grover did not leave the issue there and eventually concluded that "Joseph's band do not desire Wallowa Valley for a reservation and a home."[18]

Grover's blatant disregard for the truth in his attempt to return the Wallowa Valley to the public domain undoubtedly appealed on many levels to the federal government. The first would have been the elections the following year (1874). If Grover and the federal government were not sensitive to the demands of the white population, their positions might be sacrificed to an angry electorate. A second issue was money. In 1873 the United States entered into an economic depression. To establish settlements in the western frontier, the federal government had been compelled over the years to agree to expensive and at times disastrous treaties with the Indians, all of which seemed unpopular with the white population of the nation. Because of this lack of public support for the treaties, when fulfillment of their provisions became inconvenient, often the promises were forgotten, and hostilities between Americans and Native Americans resulted.

## Placement of Troops in the Valley

To forestall hostility or quell violence, the federal government placed military troops in the affected areas. The placement of troops was expensive and occasionally fraught with disaster, such as with the massacre of General George Custer at the Battle of the Little Big Horn in 1876. Additionally, the protection they provided to the fledgling white settlements was often inconsistent because of a lack of manpower and the massive amount of land they had been called upon to patrol. However, in areas where a large white population resided, Indian depredations or conflicts were virtually absent, not because the two cultural groups had reached a middle ground in their relationship, but because the overwhelming number of white residents marginalized the native residents and forced them from their lands.

For the nation as a whole, increased settlements provided a net cost savings and were more effective overall in establishing white control of an area. For a government and a nation unwilling to make concessions to the native inhabitants of the land, more settlement meant less trouble, and less trouble meant less money spent controlling what many at the time called the "Indian problem." Additionally, the white settlements generated revenue for the government and expanded American civilization and ideas, whereas the Indian reservations did not. Grover's outright lies about the Wallowa Valley and Joseph's band would have had considerable appeal to a nation locked in economic and social uncertainty.

## Joseph's Rejection of the Government's Mandate

In March 1873, the commissioner of Indian Affairs could no longer ignore the issues that surrounded the Wallowa Valley and other areas of the Pacific Northwest. To gain greater insight into the issues and assess the threat truly posed by the Indians, Edward P. Smith appointed a commission to investigate. By early August, these commissioners were at Lapwai and there met briefly with Joseph. The commissioners were confronted not with a savage, uncivilized man, but a well-spoken, intelligent, and sincere leader of the Nez Perce.

When the commissioners asked Joseph why he did not want schools or churches in the valley of his people, he replied that those symbols of American progress and culture would teach the Nez Perce "to quarrel about God, as the Catholics and Protestants do on the Nez Perce reservation and at other places. We do not want to learn that."[19] Joseph's argument, impressed the commissioners but did little to address the larger issues that surrounded the valley.

While Joseph may have found a sympathetic ear among the commissioners, the hostility within the valley continued to grow. Desperately, Joseph sought out the advice and help of the Indian agent, John Monteith, but Monteith was ill disposed to listen to Joseph's complaints. Joseph's refusal to confine his people on the reservation and his rejection of American religion had fueled much of the discontent that Monteith was being called upon to address. Aside from Joseph's complaints, Monteith also found himself largely the target of the settler's anger at the unpopular decisions of the federal government. Besieged and unhappy, Monteith blamed Joseph for all the problems in the valley and insisted that he and his band should enter a reservation in Idaho, by force if necessary. Angrily, Joseph left the valley and moved his people into their winter settlement.

## Entrance of Oliver Otis Howard into the Conflict

By the spring of 1874, the issues that had plagued the valley were no better and were soon to get a lot worse. The diverse issues that were represented in the struggle for the Wallowa Valley were beginning to come to a head. While national finances and upcoming elections occupied the federal government, the state government concerned itself with increasing settlement in the territory. On the Lapwai Reservation, Monteith served as a lighting rod for disputes between the Indians and the settlers. All that was needed was a final spark that would ignite these simmering issues into an explosive war. That final spark came with the appointment of Oliver Otis Howard as Commander of the Department of the Columbia.

Howard was a career military man who had graduated from West Point in 1854, and while serving in Florida during the Seminole Indian Wars, he had experienced a religious awakening that would color his attitude toward the world around him for the rest of his life. While serving in the U.S. Army during the Civil War, Howard managed to mesh together the military and religious aspects of his personality when he insisted that his troops attend prayer and temperance meetings; this feat earned him the nickname, "the Christian General." For those who found themselves under the control of General Howard, his religiosity could foster pompous and dictatorial behavior that many resented.

When Howard left his home in the East during the summer of 1874 to take up his duties in Oregon, he entered into a state whose population tottered slightly above 90,000 and boasted only 8,000 people in its largest city, Portland. As he and his family settled into the fledgling city, Howard noted that it was filled with "much wickedness" and focused his attention on elevating the moral standing of the region by expanding the role of the church and its related organizations.[20] Clearly, Joseph's belief that much of the squabbling that plagued the region came from religious beliefs of the white man would not be well accepted by the new military commander of the plateau.

As the commander of the Columbia, Howard was responsible for the safety and well-being of the white and red residents in a vast territory that stretched through Washington and Oregon into parts of Idaho and the Territory of Alaska. To accomplish this feat, he had about 1,000 troops under his command and was not unaware of the problems that he faced. In his autobiography, Howard noted that he had "inherited quite a number of Indian troubles which unless well handled would lead to war."[21] To address these "troubles," Howard called upon his aide, Major Henry Clay Wood, to review the issues that underlay the Nez Perce and settler complaints.

In his study, Wood clearly determined that Joseph's claim to the Wallowa Valley was legitimate, a position initially adopted by Howard. Based on this position, Howard wrote in his reports that he believed "it is a great mistake to take from Joseph and his band of Nez Perces Indians that valley. The white people really do not want it."[22] Sadly, Howard would abandon this initial belief when trouble arose. While severely undermanned in relation to the vast expanses he had been called upon to manage, it was perhaps Howard's belief in his own moral certitude that would prove to be the most significant factor in expanding the growing crisis in the Northwest. Howard's behavior toward the Nez Perce was paternalistic and insulting. His inability to view the larger issues outside of his own belief system and his unrealistic solutions to the situation as a whole would push the region into war.

**The First Meeting between Howard and Joseph.**   Howard's first meeting with Joseph occurred on the Umatilla Reservation in early 1875, six months after he assumed his command. He came away from the meeting impressed with the solemnity of the Nez Perce leader. Through an interpreter, Joseph asked Howard only one question, would the executive order reservation be preserved, or would the government renege on another promise to his people? Howard truthfully answered that he had heard nothing from Washington regarding the matter, and the meeting ended shortly afterward. Despite the limited communication between them, Howard came away from the meeting with the impression that he and Joseph "became quite good friends" and that Joseph would comply with the government's demands.[23] He could not have been more mistaken.

A few months after their meeting Joseph learned that the government's promise had indeed been rescinded. On June 10, 1875, Grant revoked the executive order that had established the Wallowa Valley as part of the Nez Perce reservation. Agent Monteith called Joseph to the Lapwai agency to inform him of the loss of the valley and to encourage him to bring his people onto the reservation. Predictably, Joseph "was inclined to be ugly and returned to his camp very much dissatisfied"[24] at the agent's suggestion. Fearful that the Indians might resort to violence, Monteith requested Howard send troops into the valley.

## The Council for War or Peace

Following his meeting with Monteith, Joseph called a council of the nontreaty Indians to discuss their options. At the fork of the Wallowa and Lostine rivers, near where he had buried his father, Joseph; *Tip-yah-lan-ah Ka-ou-pu*, or "Eagle from the Light"; *Peo-peo Kis-kiok Hi-hih*, or "White Bird"; Looking Glass; *Toohoolhoolzote*; and other leaders gathered to discuss their options. While Toohoolhoolzote, Eagle from the Light, and White Bird called for war, Joseph, his brother Ollokot, and Looking Glass counseled peace. As the leader of the warriors, and Joseph's most trusted counselor, Ollokot's voice carried great weight in the discussions.

*Ollokot, brother of Chief Joseph, ca. 1877. Ollokot was Joseph's most trusted advisor and supporter. He died in the last days of the Nez Perce flight at the Battle of Bear Paw Mountain. Reproduction number NA 878. Courtesy University of Washington Libraries.*

With the combined might of Looking Glass, who was also one of the great warriors of the group, Joseph's argument prevailed, and the chiefs agreed not to go to war against the whites. However, this concession was not universally embraced by several of the young braves, and Joseph acknowledged, "Our young men were quick tempered, and I have had great trouble in keeping them from doing rash thing."[25] Despite the difficulty in controlling the passion of the young warriors, Joseph was able to keep them in check; however, it seemed the government was intent on war. In the summer of 1875, the government rejected all questions about the validity of the 1863 Thief Treaty and gave approval for a wagon road to be constructed through the valley. Again, Joseph protested; however, with the troops in the valley, Joseph continued to council peace, and the construction proceeded as planned.

## THE OUTBREAK OF WAR

Because of the heightened tension in the Wallowa Valley, only five more settlers came into the territory, and by the late fall, Joseph led his band back into the protected canyons to wait out the winter. By March 1876, Joseph and his band had left their mountain retreat and had taken up temporary residence on the Umatilla Reservation in order to spend time with their extended families. While they caused no problems, the presence of Joseph and his people near the settlements caused considerable anxiety among the white population. By early summer, Joseph and his band had returned to the pastures of the Wallowa Valley in order to collect the camas roots they would need to sustain themselves through the winter ahead. It was here that the final spark that ignited the Nez Perce War occurred.

On June 22, 1876, rancher A. B. Findley discovered five of his horses missing. After a prolonged search, he came upon tracks that he assumed belonged to his horses and followed the trail to an Indian hunting camp. Believing the Indians had stolen his stock but unable to locate them in the surrounding terrain, Findley returned to his ranch and enlisted the assistance of two brothers, Wells and Oren McNall. The McNall brothers were well known in the valley, and were equally as well known to hate Indians. They returned with Findley that afternoon to await the return of the hunting party. When evening came and the Indians still had not returned, the three men returned to the settlement intent on resuming their hunt the next day.

The following day, Wells McNall and Findley rode out to the Indian camp and came upon eight braves. When the white men were spotted, seven of the braves mounted their horses and rode away, only one remained, one of Joseph's closest friends, *Wilhautyah*, or "Blowing Wind." Why Wilhautyah did not leave with the other braves remains a mystery. While several accounts of the events surrounding his death have survived, none corroborates the other. According to one of the Nez Perce witnesses, two white men came upon two Indian braves who were resting following a hunt. They disarmed the Indians and then accused them of stealing their livestock. When the Indians denied the accusation, the white men began abusing the Indians. Wilhautyah then came upon the scene and attempted to stop the violence. He quickly got the better of one of the white men, but the white man's companion shot him to death. Another account has Wilhautyah alone in the camp and preparing to dress a deer when he was shot by the white men. Still another account insists that when the seven other Indians left the camp, the two white men feared they would not be able to retrieve their stock, and Wells McNall leapt from his horse and seized Wilhautyah before he too could escape. The two men struggled, and Findley shot Wilhautyah to protect McNall, who was losing the fight. While too much time has passed to accurately discern what happened that day, the aftermath of Wilhautyah's death is a different matter.

## The Failure of the White Courts to Protect the Indians

In a panic, the remaining Indians left the scene, and soon word of the killing reached Joseph. Angered over the senseless loss of his friend, Joseph and his people buried the young warrior and listened to the increasing calls for war. Yet, despite the painful loss of his friend, Joseph continued to counsel for peace. About a week after the murder of Wilhautyah, Agent Monteith sent word that he too had heard of the killing and asked Joseph to come to him at the Lapwai agency. Joseph agreed, and the two met in early July. There Joseph related what the Indian witnesses had told him, and Monteith offered reassurances that the white authorities would deal with the killers. Fearing that Joseph would not be able to control his people, Monteith also informed Howard of the killing and requested he send troops to the area to head off any problems that may occur from the "willful and deliberate" murder of the young brave.[26]

Despite the promises of Monteith and his assertion that Wilhautyah's death had been murder, weeks passed and no arrests were made. Instead, one month after Wilhautyah's death, Joseph and his brother Ollokot were summoned to meet with Howard's aide Major Wood at the Lapwai agency. Angry that the murderers had not been arrested and that it appeared the white man's laws did not extend to the protection of the Indians, Joseph began to speak of dealing with the murder in accordance with Indian tradition. Wood sympathetically listened to Joseph's complaints and encouraged him to be patient. Wood insisted that Howard had recommended a separate commission be called that would deal with all of the issues that confronted Joseph and his people. However, such a commission would not be called if the Indians devolved into hostility. Wood offered reassurances that the white courts would deal with the murders.

For Joseph, Wood's reassurances brought the potential for the resolution of all of the difficulties that had confronted his band since the signing of the Thief Treaty 12 years earlier, and he agreed to the major's proposal. Aware that charges had not been filed against the two murderers, Howard, in a sign of good faith, encouraged the district court to file charges against Findley and McNall. By late summer, however, no charges had been filed, and Joseph began to lose patience with the white men in his valley. By the end of August, Joseph began his own investigation into the killing, first visiting Findley's home and asking to hear his side of the story. And then on September 1, he and other members of his tribe visited several of the homes of white settlers and ordered them to bring McNall and Findley to a council meeting the following day.

## Standoff at the White Settlements

The settlers refused to give up McNall and Findley, but several did attend the council and there Joseph ordered them to leave his valley by the following Sunday and insisted that the killers be given up to his people for trial. The settlers predictably refused, and the council ended. The following day, settlers reported 60–70 Nez Perce warriors led by

Joseph and Ollokot had surrounded the McNall homestead. Despite a standoff that lasted into the evening, the accused remained protected by the other white settlers, and Joseph reiterated his demand that the settlers leave the valley, or the Nez Perce would destroy their farms and drive them out forcibly.

As Joseph's deadline for the evacuation approached, the settlers sent out an alarm, and men from the surrounding communities and troops under the command of Lieutenant Albert Forse from Fort Walla Walla were dispatched to the area. Forse met with Joseph, and the two agreed not to pursue hostilities if the whites would address the murder of Wilhautyah. The following day, Forse sent word to McNall and Findley asking them to surrender to authorities as the safety of all the residents in the valley depended on their actions.

## The Trial of A. B. Findley

On September 14, both men appeared in court, and Findley was charged with manslaughter but released after posting $250 in bail. No charges were filed against McNall as he insisted he had been defending himself. During Findley's trial, the Indian witnesses who had been brought to testify were never called on. After a brief hearing, the charges against Findley were dismissed when the court ruled he had acted in self-defense. The following month, Findley insisted on having his case heard before the grand jury, but again, when no Indian witnesses were called, he was exonerated.

## Howard's Commission

The sham trial of A. B. Findley could have sparked a general uprising in the valley had Joseph not learned of Howard's efforts to secure a commission to address all of the complaints of the Wallowa Nez Perce. Satisfied that the commission would find in his favor, Joseph was able to quiet the demands for blood among his people, and this allowed Howard to secure his promised commission in October 1876. The three commissioners, David Jerome, A. C. Barstow, and William Stickney, had no experience in dealing with the Indians in the Pacific Northwest, and their appointment came at a time when Americans had little interest in granting concessions to Indians.

While the events in the Wallowa Valley had been unfolding, the nation became aware of the massacre of the Seventh Cavalry at the hands of Sioux Chief Sitting Bull in late June of that same year. With no experience in dealing with the Indians or familiarity of the events they were charged to investigate, Howard's commission, as Joseph would soon discover, was little more than a sham. On November 7, the commissioners arrived at the Lapwai agency, and a week later, Joseph, Ollokot, and about 60 warriors arrived at the council. Their entrance had been preceded almost a week earlier by the treaty Nez Perce who had liberally been sharing their complaints with the commission.

As the council got underway, Joseph was shocked to hear the opening statements of the commissioners, each of whom insisted that the Nez Perce abandon the Wallowa Valley and move onto the reservation. Instead of confirming Joseph's contention that the 1863 Thief Treaty was invalid, they insisted it was valid and binding on all the Nez Perce. The commissioners then dismissed Joseph's complaints about the settlers and maintained that the federal government could not intercede for the Indians because the Wallowa Valley belonged to the state of Oregon.

While undoubtedly stunned, Joseph was not silent on the matter before him. Six years earlier he had promised his father to protect the land of his forefathers, and he intended to keep his promise. When time came for him to speak, Joseph rose to his feet and addressed the commissioner's directive to leave his home. Though paraphrased in the commission report, the eloquence of Joseph's words can still be heard: "The earth was his mother. He was made of the earth and grew up on its bosom. The earth, as his mother was sacred to his affections, too sacred to be valued by, or sold for silver or gold. He could not consent to sever his affections from the land that bore him."[27] When Joseph further denied the authority of the federal government over his people, the commissioners and General Howard were clearly angered. They had been unable to convince the Wallowa Nez Perce to bend to their will. Howard would later insist that Joseph and his people had been "offered everything they wanted, if they would simply submit to the authority and government of the United States agents."[28] Everything, perhaps, except their land and their freedom.

As a man of devout Christian beliefs, Howard came to believe that Joseph's resistance stemmed from the influence of the Dreamer shamans whose influence prevented Joseph from being reasonable. When the commission made its recommendations to Washington, included was a suggestion that those shamans who practiced the Dreamer religion should be confined to their own agencies and their teachings suppressed, or that they be exiled to the Indian Territory. Additionally, the Nez Perce, if they did not move "within a reasonable time . . . should be placed by force on the Nez Perce reservation" in Idaho.[29] To ensure that no hostilities erupted in the valley while the removal of the Indians was taking place, the army should remain in the valley until all danger had passed. Unable to sway the commissioners, Joseph and his band left the Lapwai agency and entered the Imnaha Valley to spend the winter, unaware this would be their last in the land of their forefathers.

## NOTES

1. Josephy, *The Nez Perce*, 328.

2. Joseph, *That All People May Be One People*, 9.

3. Ibid.

4. Ibid., 6.

5. Ibid.

6. Clifford M. Drury, *Chief Lawyer of the Nez Perce Indians*. (Glendale, CA: The Arthur H. Clark Company, 1979), 229–30.

7. Joseph, *That All People May Be One People*, 10.

8. Ibid., 8.

9. Ibid., 11.

10. Josephy, *The Nez Perce*.

11. Joseph, *That All People May Be One People*, 14.

12. Ibid., 12.

13. Mark Herbert Brown, *The Flight of the Nez Perce* (Lincoln: University of Nebraska Press, 1982), 38.

14. Josephy, *The Nez Perce*, 457.

15. Brown, *The Flight of the Nez Perce*, 39.

16. Josephy, *The Nez Perce*, 463.

17. Brown, *The Flight of the Nez Perce*, 43.

18. LaFayette F. Grover, Governor of Oregon, to Columbus Delano, Secretary of the Interior, July 21, 1873.

19. Josephy, *The Nez Perce*, 461.

20. John Carpenter, *Sword and Olive Branch: Oliver Otis Howard* (New York: Fordham University Press, 1999), 244.

21. Oliver Otis Howard, *Autobiography of Oliver Otis Howard, Major-General, United States Army* (New York: Baker & Taylor, 1908), 464.

22. Candy Moulton, *Chief Joseph: Guardian of the People* (New York: Macmillan), 89.

23. Oliver Otis Howard, *Nez Perce Joseph: An Account of His Ancestors, His Lands, His Confederates, His Enemies, His Murders, His War, His Pursuit And Capture* (New York: Lee & Shephard, 1881), 29.

24. Josephy, *The Nez Perce*, 467.

25. Joseph, *That All People May Be One People*, 14.

26. Josephy, *The Nez Perce*, 473.

27. Ibid., 488.

28. Ibid., 488.

29. Ibid., 489.

# Chapter 4

# THE FLIGHT OF
# THE NEZ PERCE

## THE PLAN TO RELOCATE JOSEPH'S PEOPLE

On January 6, 1877, the new commissioner of Indian Affairs, J. Q. Smith, instructed agent Monteith to begin implementing the recommendations of the commission. Joseph and his band would be required to move onto the reservation "at once." The military would be requested to permanently station troops in the valley "in the interests of peace."[1] Monteith dispatched four treaty Indians—Joseph's brother-in-law and nephew, Reuben and James Reuben; his father-in-law, Whisk-tasket; and *Jokais*, or "Captain John"—to Joseph's camp to inform him that he was required to surrender to the reservation by April 1 of that year.

Despite Monteith's smug assurance that Joseph and his band would now be forced to comply with the demands of the government and would soon be under his control, when the four delegates returned, they reported that Joseph was unmovable in his insistence not to leave the land of his father. Monteith lost no time in writing to J. Q. Smith with the request that the military step in and compel Joseph to relinquish his lands, by force if necessary. "I think, from Joseph's actions, he will not come on the reserve until compelled to,"[2] he concluded. While the request was made to use the military to compel the Wallowa Valley Nez Perce to relocate onto the reservation, the military was reluctant to push the issue into an all-out war.

Manpower in the region was limited, and after the disaster with Custer's troops the previous summer, the military could ill afford another costly failure. Instead, Howard was advised by his superiors that it was of "paramount importance that none of the responsibility of any step which may lead to hostilities shall be initiated by the military authorities."[3] Howard was to support the Department of the Interior in the management of the Indians, but not to aggressively promote their cause. To achieve this mandate, Howard ordered that the troops remain in the Wallowa Valley until further notice.

Unfortunately, the decision to leave troops in the valley was perceived by the local newspapers and settlers in a much different way than had been intended. Rumors that the military was about to launch an offensive attack against the Nez Perce raced through the region. The once peaceful valley was again abuzz with talk of war. Howard, now concerned that talk of war could easily turn into action, ordered two more cavalry units into the valley to support the troops already there in a move that would have seemingly confirmed to the Nez Perce and the settlers that a war was in the offing.

## JOSEPH'S DESIRE FOR PEACE

Joseph and his people did not want war, only to be left in peace. The government's insistence that they owned the land of his fathers made no sense to him. The statements made by the government's agents over the years were not proof that the land had been sold. Neither he nor his father had sold the land, and Joseph had never accepted anything from the government in order to ensure that there would ever be a reason to believe that an exchange had taken place. A lie, no matter how many times it was repeated, did not make it true.

Yet, despite the unmistakable logic of Joseph's position, the government remained steadfast in its opinion and now appeared ready to use force to remove him from his land. On March 17, Joseph sent Ollokot to the Lapwai agency to ask Monteith to arrange a meeting with General Howard. At the same time, he asked Young Chief, a Cayuse chief on the Umatilla Reservation, to make a similar request of their agent,

Major Cornoyer. Monteith, sensing the opportunity to finally have Joseph under his control, did little to advance Joseph's request. However, Cornoyer did, and a council meeting was arranged between the Nez Perce and Lieutenant William Boyle on the Umatilla Reservation.

On April 1, Ollokot and several other prominent Indians from the band met at the Umatilla agency, but little came of the meeting. A second meeting slated for April 20 was to take place at Fort Walla Walla and would include Joseph and Howard. However, on the appointed day, Ollokot again appeared as a representative of his people and explained that Joseph was too ill to travel to the meeting. However, he was there to speak for him. Ollokot suggested the Umatilla join with the Nez Perce in the Wallowa Valley and surrender the Umatilla Reservation to the white man. This would allow the Nez Perce to remain on their traditional lands, and the Umatilla would be safe in the protected valley. Howard rejected the idea but established another date to meet with Joseph in two weeks, on May 3, at the Lapwai agency. With the council thus ended, Ollokot was forced to bring the disappointing news to his brother.

## Howard's Preparation for the Lapwai Peace Conference

The day prior to the meeting, Howard arrived at the Lapwai agency and began to make plans for what was to follow. He was determined that the Nez Perce would comply with the demands of the white authorities, by force if necessary. He had ordered additional troops into the valley and was prepared to use those troops to insist that the Nez Perce bend to his will. Following the conference, Howard wrote to the secretary of war and noted that "obedience was required"[4] of the Indians.

The following day, Joseph and more than 50 members of his band arrived and entered a tent that had been raised to accommodate the participants of the council. Missing from the proceedings, however, were the other bands of nontreaty Indians. The trails surrounding the agency were slippery and still wet from the spring rains, and travel along them could be torturous and time consuming. Joseph did not want to start the proceedings without their support. However, Howard was not in a mood to wait and advised Joseph that "the Indians were to obey the orders of the government of the United States."[5]

Monteith spoke next and insisted that the time had come for the Indians to submit to his authority and move onto the Lapwai Reservation.
To ensure their compliance, the military would use its soldiers, if the
tribes continued to resist. To the Nez Perce who were present, the peace
conference seemed to be scarcely more than another opportunity for the
government to dictate to the Indians. When Joseph and the headmen
of his band persisted in presenting their side of the argument, Howard
warned them not to speak to him in an insulting manner or he would
have them arrested and sent away to the Indian Territory in Oklahoma.
On this sour note, the council was adjourned until the next day in order
to allow the other nontreaty Indians time to arrive.

### Toohoolhoolzote and the Arrival
### of the Nontreaty Indians

The following morning, White Bird, Toohoolhoolzote, and Looking
Glass arrived with their respective bands. None of the chiefs wanted
war, only to be left in peace on their lands. When the council convened,
Toohoolhoolzote rose to speak for the Nez Perce. He acknowledged the
1863 Thief Treaty but insisted that since none of the bands present had
signed the treaty, it did not apply to them. In a condescending tone,
Howard responded that the nontreaty Indians, while nonsignatories to
the treaty, were still bound by it. Offended by Howard's remark and de-
meanor, Toohoolhoolzote rebuked Howard for his behavior and insisted
that he and his people be treated as men, not children. As Toohoolhoolzote spoke, the other council members nodded and voiced their approval
of his words, and those Indians who had remained outside the council
tent began to press inward in a show of support.

The white officers present began to feel acutely uncomfortable when
they realized how precarious their position was. They were surrounded
by Indians, and their support troops were not present at the council site.
When Toohoolhoolzote had finished speaking, Joseph requested a post-
ponement of the proceedings, and Howard happily agreed and suggested
that they meet again in three days. Seeing this as an opportunity to allow
the rest of the nontreaty Indians to arrive, Joseph agreed and the meeting was adjourned. Howard, however, did not agree to the adjournment

in order to benefit the Nez Perce. During the hiatus from the council, he ordered more troops from Fort Walla Walla to move into position near Lapwai lest any hostilities erupt.

In the ensuing days, rumors of war flowed freely through the valley and kept the frayed nerves of the settlers and soldiers on edge. Many of these rumors were started by Christianized Nez Perce who reported that the nontreaty bands were singing war songs. For the Christianized Indians, the opportunity to force their brethren into compliance with their beliefs was the driving force behind their actions. If the nontreaty Indians converted to Christianity and moved onto the reservation, their status would be lower than the Indians who were already there, and thus the Christianized Indians would have authority over them. As more bands of nontreaty Nez Perce filtered into the Lapwai agency, including several bands of Palouse Indians, this seemed to confirm the speculation that a general Indian war was in the offing.

***Toohoolhoolzote's Confrontation with Howard.*** When the council reconvened, Toohoolhoolzote again rose to speak but was stopped by Howard, who would later describe the old shaman in a letter to the secretary of war as a "large thick necked, ugly, obstinate savage of the worst type," who had become "more impudent in his abruptness of manner than before."[6] Howard's childish name calling did little to encourage improved relations between the Indian delegates and their white counterparts. Howard's curt dismissal of a respected chief drew an angry response from Toohoolhoolzote, and the other Indians present. Finally, Howard demanded the old Indian submit to his authority. Unbowed, Toohoolhoolzote remained defiant, and according to Joseph, demanded:

> Who are you that you ask us to talk and then tell me I shan't talk. Are you the Great Spirit? Did you make the world? Did you make the sun? Did you make the rivers to run for us to drink? Did you make the grass to grow? Did you make all these things that you talk to us as though we were boys? If you did, then you have the right to talk as you did.[7]

Toohoolhoolzote's rebuke incensed Howard, and he threatened to send the old chief to the Indian Territory, even if the process took him "years and years."[8] As if to do so immediately, Howard seized Toohool-hoolzote by the arm and led him to the guardhouse. In a move that Howard might have assumed reinforced his authority, especially since the other Indian delegates watched the exchange in stunned silence, it was actually a disastrous violation of Nez Perce diplomacy. As *Hemene Moxmox*, or "Yellow Wolf," one of Chief Joseph's nephews noted, Howard had "showed the rifle."[9] Joseph remained silent, not because he agreed with Howard, but because he was not willing to let the negotiations devolve into a blood bath.[10] As he later reported, "My men whispered among themselves whether they would let this thing be done. I counseled them to submit. I knew if we resisted that all the white men present, including General Howard, would be killed in a moment, and we would be blamed."[11] The choices for the nontreaty Indians was now clear, move onto the reservation or go to war.

## General Howard's Mismanagement of the Council Proceedings

Over the next several days, Howard collected Joseph, Looking Glass, and White Bird and rode over the Lapwai Reservation in order to choose a permanent site where the Indians would dwell. By May 12, the men returned to camp and learned that several additional troops had entered the valley. While these troops were responding to the orders that Howard had given a week earlier, to the Nez Perce the specter of war grew even larger. Chief Joseph recalled that he had "been informed by men who do not lie that General Howard sent a letter that night telling the soldiers at Walla Walla to go to Wallowa Valley and drive us out upon our return home."[12]

Two days later on May 14, Howard called a final meeting of the nontreaty chiefs and announced that they would be given 30 days to make their way to the sites that had been chosen for them. In a gesture of goodwill, he released Toohoolhoolzote from the guardhouse. Joseph and several of the other chiefs protested the timetable Howard had imposed. The rivers were still swollen, and many of the cattle and horses in their herds had recently given birth and were scattered around the country. Such a journey would be difficult in the best of times, and impossible with young animals and swollen rivers to contend with. Despite the logic of this argument, Howard remained adamant. If the Indians were not on the reservation within 30 days, they would be considered hostile, and "the soldiers will be there to drive you onto the reservation and all your cattle and horses outside the reservation at that time will fall into the hands of the white men."[13]

## GROWING ANGER IN THE NEZ PERCE CAMPS

Joseph returned to his people and was forced to confront the growing hostility of his people toward the white man. Joseph still did not want war and maintained, "I would rather give up my country. I would rather give up my father's grave. I would give up everything rather than have the blood of white men upon the hands of my people."[14] His position was becoming increasingly more difficult to maintain. A council was held, and while Toohoolhoolzote advocated for war, Joseph's position for peace prevailed.

Over the next several days, the Nez Perce began the laborious process of rounding up their stock and driving them into the lower Imhana Valley where they would be forced to cross the Snake River. While the Indians began the herculean task of moving all their possessions and stock over miles of rugged terrain, Howard sent word to the settlers to evacuate the valley until the Indians were safely on the reservation. His order only added to the fear that permeated the region, as settlers assumed they were being removed in order to not be caught between the military and the Indians when the hostilities erupted. The Indians had little time to worry about Howard's orders, for they were in a race against time.

### Crossing the Snake and Salmon Rivers

After several days of searching the high mountain passes for their stock, the Nez Perce began to move the herds toward the valleys below. In the high mountains, they struggled to ford rivers that were swollen by the melting snow, but largely they were successful in their attempts. However, by the time the Nez Perce reached the Snake River, it was a raging torrent of white water. Over two days, the Nez Perce and their stock crossed the river. While they managed to cross in safety, the tribe lost several hundred head of stock and many of their possessions in the attempt.

The band pressed forward, but before reaching the Salmon River, they paused to allow their stock to graze under the watchful eyes of their herders while the rest of the band moved on to Rocky Canyon.

## The Last Grand Council

At a placed called *Tepahlewam*, or "Split Rocks," they halted their advance and over the next 10 days held a grand council with the other nontreaty Indians in order to rest and prepare themselves for their lives on the reservation. The council began on June 2, which was 12 days before Howard's deadline to present themselves to the reservation. More than 600 men, women, and children gathered for a last moment of freedom and to enjoy the old ways. With such a large gathering, discussions turned to the treatment the Nez Perce and Palouse had been forced to endure by the white man. Soon discussion turned to anger, and talk of war began to pepper the air.

On June 12, a war parade was staged through the camp, and during the procession, the horse of a young brave named *Wahkitits*, or "Shore Crossing," stumbled on some kouse roots that had been left out to dry. The infraction was noted by the owner of the roots, a man called "Yellow Grizzly Bear," who chastised the young man for his clumsiness and then insulted him by demanding he leave the parade since he was not a warrior, because he had not avenged his father's murder at the hands of white men two years earlier. Yellow Grizzly Bear's words hurt Wahkitits deeply. The next morning, Wahkitits; *Sarpsis Ilppilp*, or "Red Moccasin Tops"; and *Wetyetmas Wyakaikt*, or "Swan Necklace," left the camp to seek revenge.

## Wahkitits's Quest for Revenge

Several years earlier, Wahkitits's father, *Tipyahkanah Siskan*, or "Eagle Robe," had struck up a friendship with a white settler named Larry Ott and had allowed him to settle on his land, but when Ott built a fence around Eagle Robe's garden, the Indian protested. Ott's response was to shoot his former friend. Before he died, Eagle Robe urged his son not to seek revenge by killing Ott, because to do so would bring hardship on all their people. In compliance with his father's wishes, Wahkitits agreed. No charges were ever filed, and Ott was not punished for the killing.

Now filled with a passion for revenge and angered over the imperious behavior of Howard and Monteith, the three warriors left camp. They rode to the home of Larry Ott and waited through the day to confront him, but he did not appear. Discouraged, but still filled with anger, the warriors met up with Wahkitits's wife at her camp along the Salmon River and decided on another target, Richard Devine. Devine was also a well-known Indian hater and had once killed a crippled Nez Perce named *Dakoopin* who had gone to his house seeking food. As in the case against Ott, no charges were ever filed.

The following morning, Wahkitits and Sarpsis Ilppilp broke into Devine's house, and while Swan Necklace and Wahkitits's wife remained outside, shot him to death. From there, the four rode to the farm of Henry Elfers, killed him, and then escaped with a roan stallion and several guns and ammunition. Two more white men suffered the same fate that day, Robert Bland and Henry Beckroge, and a third, Samuel Benedict, was wounded. In order to avoid involving their tribe in the killings and in what would surely be a violent aftermath, Swan Necklace was sent back to the camp at Split Rock to inform the warriors what they had done and to invite those who wanted to join them to come on the warpath.

## The Decision to Go to War

As talk of the killings spread through the camp, the Nez Perce elders and chiefs who had counseled peace were confronted with a growing demand for war. Absent from the chaos that gripped the camp that evening were Joseph and his brother. In order to provide meat to the camp, Joseph; Ollokot; Hophoponmi, Joseph's daughter; and *Wetatonmi*, Ollokot's wife, had returned to the herds along the Salmon River in order to butcher several animals. Their journey had been one of joy and sadness. Joseph's new wife, *Toma Alwawonmi*, or "Springtime," had given birth to a girl the day before, and it seemed she would be the last of the Nez Perce who would be born in freedom. As they prepared the meat for a feast that would welcome this new child into the world, talk of war was all that could be heard at the camp.

When Joseph returned to the Split Rock camp the next day, he saw that "all the lodges were moved except my brother's and my own. I saw clearly that war was upon us."[15] While warriors gathered under the

Most likely Springtime, the younger wife of Chief
Joseph. She gave birth to a daughter in the opening
days of the flight of the Nez Perce in the summer of
1877 and remained with Joseph through their years
in captivity. Reproduction number NA877.
Courtesy University of Washington Libraries.

direction of Toohoolhoolzote, the rest of the camp prepared to go into
hiding. Joseph counseled patience and insisted that they would be able
to explain to Howard what had happened and still make their way onto
the reservation. But even he realized that the time for peace was slip-
ping away. The other bands of nontreaty Indians refused to listen to
Joseph, and the camp broke apart.

   In order to ensure that Joseph and his people would not betray them
to the whites, about 35 other Indians were chosen to remain behind
with Joseph and his people. While he watched the retreating backs of
the other Nez Perce, Joseph felt a sense of profound sadness and regret.
In the future, he knew his people would suffer at the hands of the white
men. "I would have given my own life if I could have undone the kill-

ing of white men by my people,"[16] he would later say. Joseph resolutely placed the blame for the war that was to follow on the shoulders of Howard and the white government. He insisted the general should have treated Toohoolhoolzote as a man, and the other white men who had insulted and killed his people with impunity should have been brought to justice in the white courts. While he understood the anger that his people felt and even blamed the government and its representatives for the hostility between his people and the settlers, he would not justify the murderous actions of his own warriors.

## FIRST ATTACK

As the rest of the Nez Perce and Palouse Indians left Tepahlewam, Joseph and his band considered what to do. While they still wanted peace, it seemed peace would be unobtainable. That evening at about 10:00 P.M., the sound of horsemen filled the air. Yellow Wolf reported hearing the sound of a white man's voice, and then a bullet ripped through Joseph's lodge. No one was hit, and the intruders disappeared into the night.

The next day, the sound of another rifle about two miles in the distance was heard. War it seemed had come to Joseph, despite all he had done to avoid it. While the warriors protected the camp, Joseph and Ollokot ordered their people to quickly pack their things and prepare to join the other Nez Perce at *Sapachesap*, a cave on the Cottonwood Creek. When Joseph and his people arrived, they brought to four the number of bands who were now in rebellion, joining those of White Bird, Toohoolhoolzote, and *Husishusis Kute*, or "Bald Head," of the Palouse tribe. However, to assume that all the bands had joined in a unified consensus for war would be wrong. Joseph and Husishusis Kute still counseled for peace.

## THE FUGITIVE BANDS

Joseph and his band were greeted warmly by their brethren and advised that several skirmishes had occurred in the day they had been apart. One Indian had already been killed, and a group of warriors were preparing to avenge the loss of their brother. Yellow Wolf and several other warriors from Joseph's band joined in the war party. That evening another white man was killed, and Joseph and the other leaders of the Nez Perce realized that their camp was vulnerable to a retaliatory attack and decided to move farther down Cottonwood Creek and into the territory controlled by Looking Glass.

### Looking Glass's Rejection
### of the Fugitive Indians

However, before they reached his country, Looking Glass met the bands and refused them entrance to his land. He had long counseled for peace and did not want trouble to come to his people. Forced to change direction, the Nez Perce made their way toward White Bird's territory and a place known as *Lahmotta*, or "White Bird Canyon," where they arrived on June 16. As they journeyed, bands of young warriors let loose their anger on the white residents who lived in the Cottonwood area and along the Salmon River. Several of the settlers were killed, and their wagons were robbed or destroyed.

## HOWARD'S SURPRISE AT
## THE INDIANS' DEFIANCE

While Joseph and the rest of the Nez Perce people were making their way toward Lahmotta, by June 14, Howard had returned to Fort Lapwai. He had assumed that his heavy-handed approach toward the Nez Perce at the council had forced them into compliance and that they would soon arrive on the reservation. Howard was so confident of success that he had spent the weeks since the end of the council travelling to several of the tribes in the Columbia Plateau and bullying them into agreeing not to support Joseph or the other Nez Perce in their quest to remain outside the reservation.

Howard had intended to use Joseph's acquiescence as proof of the government's superiority; however, as reports began to come into Fort Lapwai, it was abundantly clear that the Nez Perce had not agreed to his demands. Howard, unaware that Joseph had long counseled for peace, placed the blame for the uprising squarely on his shoulders. As Joseph was one of the most articulate and intelligent of the Nez Perce leaders, Howard could not imagine anyone else marshalling his forces with greater effectiveness. No troops had been stationed along the Salmon and Cottonwood rivers, and as such, the settlers there were without the protection of the military, which made it easier for the Indians to attack. Instead of repositioning his troops after the council had broken up, Howard left his troops where he had originally placed them, where now they were helpless to assist the settlers. That evening, Howard started two companies of cavalry for the troubled region to force the Nez Perce onto the reservation and ordered more into the area from Fort Walla Walla. The troopers arrived early on June 16, but by then the violence had already grown and soon they were drawn into the growing maelstrom.

## Indian Attacks near Mount Idaho

While Howard tarried at the Lapwai Agency, roaming bands of Nez Perce warriors had attacked several wagons, including one that carried several barrels of whiskey. After killing the white teamsters, the warriors broke into the casks and liberally consumed the alcohol, adding drunkenness to the deadly mix of anger and resentment. Others ransacked homes and destroyed property. As the attacks spread, white refugees began to flood into the town of Mount Idaho. These refugees and the townsmen who heard their stories of the atrocities, like Howard, squarely placed the blame for the attacks on Joseph. Not because they had seen him in the attacks, but because his was the name most easily recalled.

## ARTHUR CHAPMAN AND THE BATTLE OF WHITE BIRD CREEK

Once the military arrived in the Mount Idaho area, the settlers convinced the commander of the troops, David Perry, that with enough guns they could eliminate the Indian menace before the Nez Perce were able to escape White Bird Canyon. The chief proponent of this plan was Arthur Chapman, a white settler who lived along White Bird Creek and who had a Umatilla wife. Chapman reported that the Indians were "cowardly" and could be easily whipped.[17] With Chapman's endorsement ringing in his ears, Perry agreed to the venture and the combined forces of the U.S. military, and the settler militia headed out. Their entrance into the area about 9:00 that evening was heralded by an Indian signal that mimicked, as one settler said, "the shivering howl of a coyote."[18]

Through that long evening, the chiefs of the various bands discussed what to do; all still wanted peace, but if attacked, they would defend their families. A multipronged response was decided upon. Six men, led by *Wettiwetti Howlis,* or "Vicious Weasel," were chosen to approach Perry's command under a flag of truce and try to arrange for peace. In the meantime, the women, children, and old men would drive the livestock into a more protected pasture while the remaining warriors would position themselves to protect the bands if the overture for peace failed. At dawn, Perry moved his combined forces toward the Nez Perce encampment and came upon the peace delegation; behind them he saw the warriors ready for battle.

Instead of slowing to address the peace delegates or even waiting for orders from David Perry, Arthur Chapman lowered his rifle and fired twice. The Indians fired in return, and the battle was on. In the melee that followed, Perry's command fell apart as the Indians attacked from all directions. By the time the battle was over, 34 troopers lay dead in the canyon, and another 4 were wounded. The Nez Perce suffered only 3 wounded, and of those, 1 was only cut by a rock during a fall. More important to the Nez Perce cause was the capture of 63 rifles and a number of pistols from the battlefield. Since most of the Nez Perce had outdated weapons or bows and arrows, the influx of weapons dramatically improved their ability to defend themselves in the event of a future attack.

## RAINBOW AND FIVE WOUNDS

The following morning, a group of warriors who had been on the plains hunting buffalo arrived in the camp. The small group included two of the greatest warriors the Nez Perce had, *Wahchumyus,* or "Rainbow," and *Pahkatos Owyeen,* or "Five Wounds." When the bands met in council that evening to discuss what to do next, it was Rainbow and Five Wounds who provided the solution. They encouraged their people to cross the Salmon River and retreat into the mountains. There, if Howard and his troops followed, they could recross the river behind the troops and then head to the Clearwater River. This would allow the Nez Perce to control when and where they would fight, and since they had only 120 warriors in the best of circumstances and more than 400 women, children, and elders to protect, any advantage they could secure would be necessary for the survival of the group. The bands agreed and crossed the river at a place called Horseshoe Bend on June 19. They left about 30 warriors behind to watch for soldiers.

As word of the Battle of White Bird Canyon began to circulate, many settlers panicked and abandoned their settlements only to crowd into the forts and towns where their numbers quickly overwhelmed the meager resources there and added to the climate of uncertainty. Those Nez Perce who had long supported the reservation and the 1863 treaty now found themselves in a difficult position. To the panicked whites, little distinction was made between a hostile Indian and a reservation Indian. Howard realized that with only two dozen men at Fort Lapwai his ability to protect the settlements was severely limited. He sent dispatches to Forts Walla Walla, Vancouver, and San Francisco requesting additional troops.

In response to Howard's requests for additional troops, the War Department dispatched units from Washington, Oregon, California, and even Alaska. Unwilling to wait for military companies that could take days or weeks to arrive, the governors of the western Pacific states called for volunteers to fill rapidly forming militia companies that would be called on to protect individual communities. As the panic spread, "hostile" Indians came to include any Indian not on a reservation, and reports of depredations increased dramatically. In all communities, it seemed the Indians with whom the whites had lived in peace had suddenly become "bloodthirsty," and subsequently, calls rose for all Indians not on reservations to be rounded up. Within the white settlements no consideration was given to the possibility that the Nez Perce were hostile or bloodthirsty because they had been forced to fight for their homes or in the defense of their lives. For all those living in terror in the white communities of the Pacific Northwest, there was one culprit for all the turmoil they were experiencing, Joseph. While Howard understood that a general Indian war was not in the offing, he too firmly believed his primary foe was Chief Joseph of the Nez Perce.

## HOWARD'S DELAY IN PURSUING THE NEZ PERCE

By June 22, reinforcements had arrived at Fort Lapwai, and Howard led almost 227 soldiers into the countryside to search for Joseph. Accompanying his force were 20 volunteers and other noncombatants. Two days later, he was at White Bird Canyon, and the Nez Perce scouts were carefully watching his movements. Most of the day, Howard's men spent scouting the area and burying the men who had fallen during the battle on June 17. Despite rumors that circulated to the contrary, none of the bodies had been mutilated. As Chief Joseph would later recount of the battle, "None of the soldiers was scalped. We do not believe in scalping nor in killing wounded men."[19] Arthur Chapman, the man whose rash action had started the battle at White Bird Creek, had signed on as a scout for Howard and with another settler named Tom Page. Together they tracked the Nez Perce to the Salmon River and reported back to Howard what they had seen.

Surprised that the Indians had successfully executed a plan to avoid the army troops, Howard noted in his report that "the leadership of Chief Joseph was indeed remarkable . . . No general could have chosen a safer position, or one that would be more likely to puzzle and obstruct a pursuing foe."[20] While camped near White Bird Canyon, Howard's troops were reinforced by an additional 175 soldiers. He now had more than 400 fighting men at his command, against a fighting force that numbered no more than 120. However, instead of immediately pursing the Nez Perce, he delayed at the edge of the Salmon for several days until he finally commenced his crossing on July 1.

## Recrossing the Salmon River

During the time he delayed at the river's edge, Howard received erroneous reports that Looking Glass had allowed his warriors to join the rebels. Concerned that Looking Glass would attack the settlements while he and his troops were searching for Joseph, Howard ordered two companies of cavalry under the command of Captain Stephen Whipple to return to the Clearwater River to arrest the chief. While Howard and his men remained at the Salmon River, the Nez Perce prepared to leave their camp and recross the river. However to get behind Howard and his troops they would need to head higher into the mountainous terrain and circle around. This would require they jettison their possessions and stock.

Caches of goods were hidden along the banks of Deer Creek as the Indians prepared for their move; when all was ready, the Nez Perce abandoned their camp. On the same day, Howard crossed the Salmon River in search of the fleeing Indians. Thirty-six hours and 25 miles later, the Indians emerged at Craig Billy Crossing and recrossed the Salmon River. As Joseph and the fleeing Nez Perce outmaneuvered Howard, trouble erupted for Looking Glass and his people.

## Attack on Looking Glass's Village

On July 1 the troops sent by Howard to arrest Looking Glass had arrived at his camp and demanded the chief surrender to them. When Looking Glass sent word that he and his people wanted nothing to do with the hostilities and refused to present himself, conditions spiraled out of control. One of the volunteers in the company fired into the camp at an Indian against whom he had a grudge, and that sparked an all-out melee. Several of Looking Glass's people were killed, but within moments, the village was abandoned.

Unwilling to give chase, the troops set fire to the lodges, trampled through the carefully tended gardens, and stole more than 700 head of stock before abandoning the now ruined village. The actions of Whipple and his command succeeded in inflaming the anger of the Indians but failed to accomplish their goal to arrest the Indian chief. Instead of pursuing Looking Glass, the troops left the village and returned to Howard's command. Whipple's foolish action added another hostile band of Indians to the mix that day and imperiled Howard's supply line to his rear.

When word of the attack on Looking Glass's camp reached Howard, he ordered Whipple to join with Perry at Cottonwood and from there protect a supply train that would reprovision Howard's growing army. On July 3, two citizen scouts under Whipple's command sighted a warrior named *Seeyokoon Ilppilp*, or "Red Spy," and attacked. One of the scouts was killed, and Red Spy pursued the other back to where Whipple and his men were waiting for Perry to appear. Unseen by the troopers, Red Spy took stock of the military camp and then returned to the main Nez Perce camp to report his findings. Whipple, upon hearing of the death of his scout, sent a dozen men under the command of Second Lieutenant Sevier Rains to scout the area and retrieve the body of the fallen scout.

## Battle at the Cottonwood

While Lieutenant Rains searched for the body of the fallen scout, Nez Perce warriors under the command of Rainbow and Five Wounds returned to where Whipple had made his camp and there came upon Rains's detachment. A brief skirmish ensued, and all the men under Rains's command were killed. When Whipple discovered the massacre, he sent word to Howard and, the following day, July 4, prepared to move the rest of his command back to Lapwai to protect the supply train that was being directed by Perry. However, before he was able to put his plan into action, the Nez Perce attacked again, but this time, the soldiers were able to dig in, and the second day of the Battle at the Cottonwood ended without further casualties. The following day, volunteers under the command of D. B. Randall came across Nez Perce who had left the main Indian camp to raid, and another skirmish ensued in which Randall and another volunteer were killed, but no Nez Perce were lost.

## Criticism against Howard Mounts

As news of the Battle at the Cottonwood began to filter in, public condemnation of Howard and the efforts of his troops were being bellowed across the Columbia Plateau. The massacres of two companies of men, especially so soon after the loss of Custer and the Seventh Cavalry, and Howard's failure to even glimpse sight of his enemy, invited scathing criticism of Howard and at times grudging praise for the man white America assumed had orchestrated the Nez Perce actions, Joseph. As one settler reported, "Chief Joseph's magnanimity may save us, and that is all."[21] Howard's losses forced him to retreat from his position, and by the time he regrouped, he was back where he had started his campaign on June 27.

While choruses of voices, including Howard's own, began to speak of a "Red Napoleon" and of the war Chief Joseph, the reality was far different. Joseph, while an important member of the council that was made up of all the chiefs of the Nez Perce bands that had taken flight, continued to press for peace. With the opinion of his people in support of war, Joseph could do nothing to dissuade them and instead assumed an ancillary role in their battles against their enemies.

## JOSEPH'S ROLE DURING THE ATTACKS

During the movement of the tribe and in battle, Joseph was responsible for the well-being of his people. This was a position of sacred trust, as the men who fought would fight only if they knew their families were protected and cared for if they fell in battle, and one that would ensure the preservation of the tribe. Joseph ensured that the wounded were cared for, that the livestock were protected and herded ahead of the tribe, and that all his people, including the widows and orphans, would not be destitute. He did not assume or aspire to join the ranks of the warriors who were ably represented by his brother, Ollokot, and Toohoolhoolzote.

As the Nez Perce settled into a temporary camp on the side of Clearwater River, they were joined by Looking Glass and his band. The addition of another 40 warriors swelled the military ranks of the Nez Perce and added another voice to the continuing chorus of war. As the Nez Perce settled into their camp, the white survivors from the Battle at Cottonwood regrouped and, under the leadership of a settler named Edward McConville, received reinforcements and reconnoitered the area. McConville's men discovered the Indian encampment and sent a message to Howard to come quickly. However, while the volunteers discovered the Nez Perce, the Nez Perce also discovered the volunteer company.

### Nez Perce Attack McConville's Volunteer Militia

On July 9 warriors led by Rainbow, Five Wounds, and Ollokot pinned the hapless volunteers down for more than a day. While no casualties resulted on either side, the swiftness with which the Indians attacked and the skill of their warriors unnerved the volunteer militia. Howard's inability to arrive at the site of the skirmish, even days later, reinforced in the minds of many of the settlers the incompetence of the U.S. Army and the military prowess of Joseph and his men. Discouraged, McConville and his men retreated to Mount Idaho.

### Nez Perce Force Howard's Retreat

Stung by the seemingly unending criticism, once Howard received McConville's message regarding the Indian encampment, he set off with a fighting force that now comprised almost 600 men. Howard's plan was to move around the eastern flank of the Indian camp and then coordinate a simultaneous attack using McConville's troops to attack from the west. When Howard and his troops came upon the Indian encampment on July 11, he was unaware that McConville had already left the area. As Howard received word that advance troops had come upon the Indian encampment, the Nez Perce were alerted to the arrival of the military and immediately swung into action. Howard was forced to react.

Nez Perce warriors swarmed through the hillsides surrounding the encampment and fired into the advancing troops. Despite outnumbering the Nez Perce warriors two to one, many of Howard's troops had never come under fire before, and with fully a quarter of his fighting force composed of volunteers, many under his command were ill trained and ill equipped. The Nez Perce barrage stopped Howard's advance in its tracks. As Howard pushed his uncoordinated attack, artillery companies manning the army's howitzer and Gatling guns became confused in the skirmish and fired on their own men. While the battle raged through the blistering hot July day, Howard and his men were prevented from advancing.

That evening as the sounds of the battlefield faded into the darkness, the chiefs met to discuss what to do next. Joseph again counseled for peace, but the war chiefs countered that if the soldiers could be wiped out the next day, the Nez Perce would be safe and would no longer need to run. Despite sharp criticism from some warriors and the noncombatant chiefs, the decision to continue to fight carried the day. The following day, Howard and his men resumed the attack from newly reinforced positions and began to push up against the Nez Perce defenses. By the afternoon of the second day, a resupply train could be seen in the distance. In order to protect the advancing train, Howard ordered troops to increase their fire against the Indian position. The massive increase in activity began to break the resilient Indian lines, and word raced back to the Indian encampment that they were in danger of being overrun.

## Battle at the Clearwater

Now that the battle threatened the village itself, Joseph sprang into action. As the one responsible for the protection of the village, its contents and his people, Joseph knew that the rapid withdrawal of the camp was the only option. He shouted at the women and children to pack up and retreat as quickly as possible. The urgency in his voice was accentuated by the sight of warriors racing into the camp to avoid the withering fire of the soldiers. Without time to pack, the Nez Perce quickly jettisoned their goods, and taking only what they could carry, they fled from the battle scene. In the chaos that ensued, Joseph instructed boys to drive as much of the herd ahead; his people would need the animals for food and transportation.

As Joseph coordinated the rapid retreat of the camp, he was unaware that his own wife and newborn child were in peril. Springtime, Joseph's

*General Oliver Otis Howard, who pursued the Nez Perce across Yellowstone in 1877. It was Howard's paternalistic and autocratic behavior that pushed the Nez Perce to flee their homelands in the summer of 1877. Photographer unknown; ca. 1909. Courtesy National Park Service.*

second wife, was unable to escape with the other women and children because the horse she was attempting to mount would not remain still enough for her to clamor aboard safely with her infant daughter. Yellow Wolf came upon the frantic mother and child and assisted her in mounting the horse, and together they made their escape. In their haste to retreat, the Nez Perce had been forced to leave behind valuable supplies, money, and food, all of which they would need in the months ahead.

Despite their success in driving the Nez Perce from the field, Howard's soldiers did not pursue the retreating Indians. Instead, they refocused their attention on looting the camp, and what they did not steal, they burned. Despite his success in forcing the Nez Perce from the battlefield, Howard's victory seemed in many ways like a defeat. Fifteen soldiers were dead, and another 25 lay wounded after 27 hours of fighting. The Nez Perce in comparison lost 4, and another 6 were wounded. Criticism of Joseph during the Battle at the Clearwater has resounded over the years, much of it stemming from a misunderstanding of the role Joseph had been called upon to play among his people. Joseph's responsibilities were for the preservation of all his people, not merely his own family. For Joseph, his fulfillment of that obligation to his people almost cost him those he held most dear.

## THOMAS SUTHERLAND

The Nez Perce retreat was aided by the greed of the settlers and soldiers who descended into the abandoned camp. Distracted by the wealth that had been left behind, the soldiers and volunteers did not pursue the Indians; this allowed the Nez Perce the opportunity to move out of harm's way and establish a new camp. The five bands headed to a Christianized settlement at Kamiah, the site where the Nez Perce were created as a people, and from there the Nez Perce would consider what to do next. In the interlude, Howard, now glowing from his first success in the campaign against the Nez Perce, lost no time in using the power of the media to remove some of the sting from the previous weeks criticism of the campaign. Howard largely turned to the pen of Thomas Sutherland to rebuild his tarnished reputation.

Sutherland was a 27-year-old recent graduate from Harvard who had embarked on a career as a journalist. He was the only journalist to follow the war to its conclusion and, in the early weeks of the campaigns, developed a warm friendship with Howard. Sutherland's sympathy and ready ear provided an outlet for General Howard to express his point of view to the press, and Sutherland did not disappoint him. Day after day in stories that were carried in the leading regional and national newspapers of the day, including the *Portland Standard*, the *New York Herald*, and the *San Francisco Chronicle*, Sutherland ensured the nation knew of Howard's exploits and of the daring foe that he faced. The stories filed by Sutherland pitted two great warriors against each other, the wily red man, Chief Joseph, and the gallant general, Oliver Otis Howard.

## KAMIAH: BACK TO THE HEART OF THE BEAST

The Nez Perce village of Kamiah was a successful Christian village. Some of the Nez Perce's most influential Christian leaders came from the village, including Lawyer's son, James, and James Reuben, the son of Old Reuben and Joseph's sister, *Elawinonmi*. They resided at a place of great spiritual significance among the Nez Perce, where the heart of the monster lay, and where the Nez Perce had become a people. However, when the nontreaty bands approached the settlement, they were denied access to the resources, fellowship, and comfort of the village.

The Christianized Nez Perce did not want to bring the wrath of the U.S. military down upon themselves. Additionally, they did not agree with the religious beliefs of their brethren, believing them to reside in spiritual darkness. Undeterred by the rejection from their brothers and sisters, the nontreaty Nez Perce established their camp across the river and developed a plan to deal with their pursuers. They would construct boats out of buffalo skins and then send their women and children across the river with their meager goods and livestock. As their families entered into the Bitterroot Mountains, they would draw the attention of the soldiers, who would likely pursue them. With the soldiers distracted by the women and children, the warriors would hide themselves along the river and ambush the soldiers when they attempted to cross.

By July 13, it seemed that their plan would work. As the soldiers appeared along the bank of the river, the Nez Perce warriors opened fire and drove them back several hundred yards. There Howard's advance troops hunkered down to await reinforcements. Despite taunts from the

Nez Perce warriors, the soldiers would not advance and when Howard came upon the scene, he ordered his troops to stay put. Howard
reckoned the tribe was heading to the Weippe Prairie, the site where
72 years earlier Lewis and Clark had first met the Nez Perce people. However, if he was able to convince the warriors that he intended to head
back toward Lapwai, perhaps he might be able to circle around and catch
them in a pincer move.

As Howard put his plan into play, the Nez Perce anticipated his movements and cut the ropes that were used by the ferry that Howard would
rely on to cross the river. Additionally, the Nez Perce decided on a ruse
of their own; they sent word back to the Christianized Nez Perce that
Joseph wished to surrender and asked to meet Howard at the river. The
weeks of battle and constant movement had been hard on his people,
and he wanted to discuss terms that would allow him and his people to
go onto the reservation.

When Howard received the message from the Christianized Nez
Perce, he returned to the river to await his meeting with Joseph. However, instead of meeting the Nez Perce leader and securing a glorious
conclusion to the struggle, Howard was greeted by a lone Indian man
named "No Heart," who waited on the opposite bank of the river. No
Heart shouted that he had been sent by Joseph who, though intent on
surrender, had been forced by the other chiefs to continue his flight. No
Heart engaged Howard for several hours in futile negotiations, before
showing his true colors. When Howard became impatient at the lack of
progress, No Heart slapped his buttocks in a sign of contempt and then
rode off into the hillside. Howard had been duped, but unwilling to let
the opportunity for a successful conclusion escape so easily, Howard remained at the edge of the river for another day in the hope that Joseph
would appear. Howard's delay allowed Joseph and the nontreaty Nez
Perce the opportunity to escape and to plan their next move.

## LOOKING GLASS ENCOURAGES
## THE NEZ PERCE TO JOIN THE CROW

After successfully eluding Howard, the Nez Perce met in council. Looking Glass proposed the tribe move into the territory of the Crow. Years
earlier, he and his warriors had aided them in a war against the Lakota,

and the Crow had sworn they would assist the Nez Perce in battle if the time ever came. In Crow country there were few white men and plenty of buffalo to hunt. They could rebuild their herds of horses and cattle in the wide open grasslands and live in peace. If the military continued to pursue them, they could head north into Canada and be far from the reach of the meddlesome Howard.

While the other chiefs embraced Looking Glass's proposal, only Joseph was hesitant. To abandon the land of their fathers meant they were abandoning the land that the Creator had given to their people. Additionally, they were not accustomed to the plains; they lived in the mountains and meadows of the Columbia Plateau. Instead, Joseph proposed they return to their lands and fight for them. Better to die in defense of their land and their way of life than to live as sojourners in the country of other people. Despite the eloquence of his words and the powerful draw of their country, the decision was made to go to the land of the Crow.

In addition to the decision to seek sanctuary among the Crow, the nontreaty Nez Perce agreed that a single leader should guide them during their flight; Looking Glass was chosen for the task. There would be no going back to the land of their fathers; now if Joseph decided to take his band away, he would forever sever the bond between his band and those who had decided to flee. For Joseph and his people, this would have left them abandoned and alone in a hostile landscape. They had no choice but to abide by the decision of the council. It therefore became an ironic twist in the story of the flight of the Nez Perce that the man the Americans had assumed was orchestrating the battles and the precision retreats was in fact compelled to follow the dictates of another chief.

## Crossing the Bitterroot Mountains

On July 16 the combined Nez Perce tribes began the long trek across the Bitterroot Mountains and into the land of the Crow. They would follow the same trail that had brought Lewis and Clark to their villages. The combined might of the five tribes was between 750 and 800 people, and they herded before them more than 3,000 horses. As they proceeded over the torturous paths that led through the mountains, Looking

Glass assigned five warriors to watch for soldiers. If any were sighted, two of the warriors would warn the tribe, and the other three would delay any advance by pinning down their enemy.

While the Nez Perce retreated into the Montana Territory, Howard was busy again with reports of Indian depredations that had occurred within the Department of the Columbia. Inclined to allow Joseph and his people to leave without further molestation, Howard was disheartened to receive orders from Commander of the Army William Tecumseh Sherman ordering him to pursue the renegades and bring them under the control of the government. Reluctantly, Howard ordered reinforcements to protect the territory and prepared to follow after the retreating Indians.

## NEZ PERCE ENTER MONTANA

Eleven days after they had entered the Bitterroot Mountain range, the Nez Perce emerged into the high meadows of Montana and exited the Lolo Trail just as Howard was preparing to enter the trail. As the Nez Perce entered the Montana Territory, their last memory of war was now two weeks behind them and many believed that Howard would not pursue them. As their herds pastured in the meadows, talk began to circulate that Joseph and White Bird might return to the Columbia Plateau after the tribes had successfully entered the land of the Crow, and hope that time would allow them to make peace. However, as they traveled from the high pastures into the foothills of Montana, their hopes that the war had been left behind evaporated.

Scouts reported that whites had established a breastwork on the trail ahead and were waiting for the Indians to appear. Looking Glass, Joseph, and White Bird went to investigate the report. When they came upon the installation, they found that the breastwork, while meager, was protected by 25 soldiers from Fort Missoula, 20 or more Flathead allies, and 150 to 200 volunteers from the surrounding countryside, many of whom knew and had traded with the Nez Perce. This saddened the Nez Perce as they counted many of the white men as their friends and the Flathead had been their allies for generations. They had hoped that their escape from Idaho would signal an end to the war, but it seemed it had followed them even into Montana.

The three Nez Perce leaders met with Captain Charles C. Rawn and advised him of their desire for peace; to Rawn, this was good news. Rawn had little stomach for a fight. His volunteers could not be relied upon in the event of a fight, and the Flathead warriors only accompanied his troops in order to avoid any repercussions from the government against their people. When the Nez Perce informed him that they wished only to travel peacefully through the land, he readily consented and allowed them to pass. As Joseph would later recount, when they came upon Rawn and his soldiers, "We made a treaty with these soldiers. We agreed not to molest anyone and they agreed that we might pass through Bitterroot country in peace. We bought provisions and traded stock with white men there. We understood that there was to be no more war.[22]

## Stevensville

Believing that peace had now been agreed to, the Indians acted accordingly. They entered into the town of Stevensville, and despite some concerns, the Nez Perce were able to convince the townspeople of their peaceful intentions. Looking Glass and the townspeople knew that the tension between them could easily erupt into fighting, something that would only make their trek more difficult. To control his warriors, Looking Glass sat atop his horse in the middle of the town's main street with his whip at the ready in case anyone within the Nez Perce bands acted foolishly. No one did, and trade continued without incident. When they left the town, the Nez Perce paraded in their finest clothing, Joseph wore a red coat emblazoned with small mirrors, a fitting garment for the "Red Napoleon."

As they traveled through the Montana Territory, their numbers swelled. A band of Nez Perce who were led by Chief Eagle from the Light had left Idaho several years earlier to live among the Flathead Indians. Some of the families who belonged to the band joined the retinue. As the Nez Perce traveled, stories of their passage took on a life of their own among the settlers in the Montana Territory. Few tales seemed to accurately reflect the peaceful intentions of the group or of their actions. Local and national newspapers continued to scream about atrocities and Indians on the warpath.

Some of these reports had a kernel of truth to them as Toohoolhool-zote's warriors had continued to raid homesteads and had attacked a few white men in the area; however, they were vastly overblown in their accuracy. As rumors spread through the white population, the Nez Perce became increasingly aware of the precariousness of their position. Criticism that Looking Glass was not taking the appropriate precautions to protect the people began to be heard. Looking Glass ignored the concerns and insisted that the war was over. He refused to move the group along at a faster pace; to do so would exhaust their meager supplies and livestock more than was necessary. Even Joseph, who could normally be counted on to err on the side of caution, was quiet on the subject. However, many within the band began to feel uneasy; their intuition would prove to be right.

## Looking Glass Ignores Concerns about the War

A few days later, the group decided to establish a camp in the Big Hole prairie, along a stream that fed a grove of trees. The rich grass would help to replenish the strength of their horses and provide them the opportunity to prepare tent poles for the winter and to dig for camas roots. Without the tent poles for their winter lodges, they would be unable to withstand the harsh Montana winter. It was now early August, and the winter would be upon them soon. With Looking Glass's continued reassurance that war had passed, Joseph took over organization of the camp. Horses were set out to graze under the watchful eyes of Indian boys, and a tent for the ill and wounded was erected.

Despite the seeming calm, the prickling feeling that things were not right continued to plague the dreams and thoughts of many of the people. A group of warriors approached Looking Glass with a proposal to backtrack and check out the trail; all they would need were a few additional horses to make the journey as their mounts were nearly exhausted. Looking Glass refused to part with any horses and dismissed their concerns. Without the additional horses they needed, the warriors abandoned their plan.

As the Nez Perce labored, they saw several white men near their camp. However, as Joseph would note, "Thinking that peace had been made, we did not molest them. We could have killed them or taken them prisoner, but we did not suspect them of being spies, which they were."[23] The men were part of a scouting party from a mixed company of 163 soldiers from the Seventh Infantry and 34 volunteers who were under the command of Colonel John Gibbon. At dawn on August 9, Gibbon ordered an attack on the still sleeping Indian camp.

## MASSACRE AT BIG HOLE

A fusillade of bullets ripped the slumbering Indians from their dreams, and instantly, the camp descended into chaos. As the soldiers kept up their firing, Indian women grabbed their children and tried to pull them to safety, while warriors searched for their weapons in the darkness of their lodges. Their desperate struggle to protect themselves was made all the harder by a growing number of fires that began to erupt as soldiers set fire to the Indian lodges. Ignoring the acrid smoke and compelled by the screams of their people, many warriors abandoned the search for weapons and attacked Gibbon's men with rocks, sticks, or their bare hands. As the camp was overwhelmed by the soldiers, women picked up the weapons of their fallen husbands and fired back into the soldiers' lines.

In the chaos, Joseph was forced from his lodge and ran to the horses to keep Gibbon's men from scattering them. Without the horses, his people would not be able to travel quickly and would be unable to carry their possessions or their wounded. When the horses were secure, he returned to the chaos, but had no weapon to defend himself or his people. Powerless before the onslaught, Joseph found shelter along the side of the creek, and there he cradled his infant daughter in his arms protecting her from the bullets that ripped through the air. Amid the chaos, he saw a warrior named "Two Moons" and called out for a weapon, but none came; all he could do was wait. After 20 minutes, the Nez Perce warriors were able to form skirmish lines and began to push back Gibbon's soldiers. In a short time, they forced the soldiers back across the creek and into a wooded area.

Once the camp was safe, Joseph moved the herd nearer to the decimated camp and began to direct his people to prepare to leave. It was uncertain how long the warriors would be able to hold back the onslaught, and they needed to move quickly. The camp was a mass of organized chaos. The dead were hastily buried amid a seemingly unending chorus of wailing and grief. Women gathered packs and stowed any goods that had not been destroyed in the fires or in the fighting. Those who were badly wounded were tied onto travois, while those who could still ride were assisted onto horses.

### Escape from Big Hole

By noon the stunned band, led by Joseph and White Bird, moved slowly across the dry prairie and toward the mountains where they hoped they would find a refuge from the horror they had just witnessed. Among the wounded was Springtime, Joseph's wife. To compound his concern, their infant daughter became ill in the mounting heat of the day. As the group journeyed toward the northeast, Joseph was forced to watch as more of his people died. He helped bury the dead, including the wife of his brother, *Aihits Palojami,* or "Fair Land."

As Joseph assigned the care of newly orphaned children to tribal members, he counted the dead; more than 90 had fallen, and more than half had been women, children, and elders. The Nez Perce losses included, Rainbow, Five Wounds, No Heart, Wahkitits, and *Hahtalekin,* the Palouse leader. Gibbon's company lost 29, with 40 wounded. As the tribe continued its plodding trek away from the carnage on the prairie, anger rose up within the group—anger at the white men, anger at Howard, and anger at Looking Glass. That evening they camped at a place called *Takseen,* or "the Willows," which was about 12 miles from Big Hole. As the camp settled into the evening, a council meeting was held, and the chiefs discussed what to do. Joseph counseled a return to their lands, but his suggestion was rejected. Looking Glass was replaced as the leader of the group by a Nez Perce warrior named Lean Elk or Poker Joe who had been among those Nez Perce of Eagle from the Light's band when they joined the refugees in the Bitterroot Valley. In addition to his prowess as a warrior, Poker Joe was half white and his ability to understand both the native and the white worlds benefited the fleeing Indians.

## POKER JOE ASSUMES COMMAND

Under the direction of Poker Joe the flight of the Nez Perce became more urgent. The people would rise at first light and begin the long trek toward the country of the Crow. Warriors were assigned to move in front of or behind the group to provide the maximum protection to the women and children. Fires were kept at a minimum. Food, lodge poles, buffalo robes, and clothing were all in short supply. As the wounded died or the weak succumbed to the strain of the trail, they were quickly buried, and the group moved on. Orphaned children were assigned to new families, and far too often the aged chose to be left behind to fend for themselves rather than slowing the entire group. All of these things Joseph managed and arranged, amid the increasing sorrow of his people and the increasing anger of their warriors.

Desperate to feed their families and to assuage their anger, the warriors spread into the surrounding countryside and attacked isolated homesteads and freight wagons with abandon. Settlers were slaughtered, and their goods taken. Panic again gripped the countryside. Rumors that the Nez Perce were moving to join Sitting Bull, the architect of Custer's defeat the year before, and to join in a general Indian war spread like wildfire. At the head of this marauding band of savages, the public could see only Joseph. While the reports of atrocities increased, so too did criticism against the military.

## BLACK HAIR'S VISION

Six days after the massacre at Big Hole, General Howard had closed the gap between the Nez Perce and his army. Pursued to the point of exhaustion, the Nez Perce decided to listen to a vision that a man named Black Hair had had the night before: he had seen the warriors going back over the trail they had just crossed and coming back with the horses from Howard's camp. So 28 warriors including Ollokot, Toohoolhoolzote, and Looking Glass retraced their steps. After midnight the warriors snuck into Howard's herds and stampeded more then 200 mules and a smattering of horses. While the intent of their raid had been to steal the horses used by Howard's cavalry in order to slow their advance, the loss of the mules proved to be almost as good. The mules carried the supplies for the advancing army and their loss hampered Howard's supply train and hence his ability to reprovision his men and continue the chase. Howard's troops pursued the retreating Nez Perce warriors, but the three companies that were sent to recover the stock were pinned down by the warriors and quickly returned.

As word of the Nez Perce raid reached the newspapers across the country, condemnation of Howard's mishandling of the war and praise for the resourcefulness of the Nez Perce, especially Chief Joseph, screamed across the headlines. A *Harper's Weekly* story from late August 1877 reported, Chief Joseph "to be a man of intelligence and strength of character. He is certainly a shrewd and active fighter, and his influence over the Indians is very great."[24] Woodcuts of a highly idealized Indian, purported to be that of Joseph, began to appear in the press along with descriptions heralding why the conflict had come to be in the first place.

The Department of the Army was left to look like a group of heavy-handed, blundering fools who had started a fight they could not finish, and in many parts of the nation, sympathy favored the fleeing Nez Perce. A frustrated William Tecumseh Sherman wrote to Howard on August 24, "that force of yours should pursue the Nez Perce to the death."[25] Washington wanted the fiasco ended, as quickly as possible, but the Nez Perce were still well out of Howard's reach. The longer the flight of the Nez Perce continued, the longer public opinion would criticize the military and the greater the chance that other hostile bands of Indians like the Sioux or the Cheyenne would join with the Nez Perce in an all-out war against the United States.

The Nez Perce continued their forced march across the Yellowstone basin and into Yellowstone Park. They came upon several campers who were startled to find themselves surrounded by the Indians. Unwilling to allow any white man to go free lest he report their whereabouts to Howard, the Nez Perce forced the white campers to come along with them. While five of the campers escaped, four remained with the Nez Perce. One of the campers, Mrs. George F. Cowen, was allowed to spend time at Joseph's camp; later she would note that Joseph was "somber and silent" despite attempts to draw him into conversation.[26] From there the group moved along the Yellowstone River and then crossed over in an attempt to put more ground between themselves and Howard's army. Once the Nez Perce crossed the river, they released their captives, unharmed. Several other tourists and campers in Yellowstone Park were not so lucky. Many members of the camping party that Mrs. Cowen had been part of were attacked by Nez Perce warriors, including her husband, who was shot and left for dead.

## THE SKIRMISH AT CANYON CREEK

By the first week of September, Howard was convinced he knew the path the Indians would take and telegraphed Colonel Samuel Sturgis and his men to head off the Nez Perce at the Shoshone River. Howard would continue his approach from the rear, and together they would trap the Nez Perce and end the national drama for good. However, the trails that the military had been following were false trails left by the wily Poker Joe, and the Indians were able to slip past. When Sturgis and Howard met again on August 11, they realized their quarry had given them the slip and were now 50 miles away and headed into the plains.

Undeterred, Howard resupplied the cavalry under Sturgis and sent him back out after the Nez Perce. A few days later, at the mouth of Canyon Creek, Sturgis's men came upon the Nez Perce trail and increased their pace in order to attack the Indians' rear. However, Sturgis's men had been sighted by the Nez Perce scouts who quickly began to prepare an attack plan of their own. The noncombatant Nez Perce were hurried into the canyon along with the horse herd, while the warriors took up positions along the bluffs to hold off the advancing troopers. Caught between the guns of the warriors, Sturgis was forced to call off the attack.

The skirmish in the mouth of Canyon Creek had significant implications for the Nez Perce. Many of Sturgis's scouts were members of the Crow nation. When the Crow joined the soldiers in their pursuit, the Nez Perce abandoned their plan to settle in the land of the Crow. Instead, they would be forced to continue their flight into Canada and seek sanctuary among the Sioux who had fled there after the Custer massacre the year before.

## THE FLIGHT TOWARD
## THE CANADIAN BORDER

By September 17, the Nez Perce crossed the Missouri River and had camped at the Mussleshell River; there they rested and held a council to decide what to do next. The border with Canada was still several hundred miles away, but the exhausting pace was beginning to show itself. At the council, Looking Glass encouraged the chiefs to consider a period of rest. He insisted that the cavalry was far behind them and the people were teetering on the verge of collapse. Their horses were equally spent, and many were too lame or worn out to continue much further. Poker Joe counseled against slackening their pace until they were over the border; only after they had crossed could they be sure they were safe. Despite the appeal of Looking Glass's position, the decision to continue to move at a rapid pace carried the day, and for the next several days, the Nez Perce closed the gap between themselves and the Canadian border.

On September 23, the exhausted bands of Nez Perce had reached Cow Island Landing along the Missouri River. There they intended to cross the river and to secure as many supplies as they could from a trade depot that was lightly guarded by settlers and about a dozen soldiers. While the warriors pinned down the guard, men and women raided the storehouse of anything they could carry. When they finished emptying the depot of what they wanted, the Nez Perce set fire to the building and the remaining goods.

The next day found the Nez Perce heading off in a northerly direction searching for a pass between the Little Rockies and Bear Paw Mountains. As they rode, they came across a wagon train and attacked, killing three of the teamsters in the process. While the warriors were looting the wagons, troops led by Major Guido Ilges came upon them and counterattacked. The warriors easily repulsed the soldiers, and Ilges was forced to retreat. Later that same day, the Nez Perce made another fateful decision. At another council of the chiefs, Looking Glass, who had lost the trust of his people and stature for the delay that had cost them so dearly at Big Hole, again insisted that the people needed to rest. He berated Poker Joe for pushing the people too hard and insisted on assuming control of the group again. Poker Joe and the other chiefs, including Joseph, acquiesced to his demand, and Looking Glass was allowed to assume command for the last time.

## LOOKING GLASS RESUMES COMMAND OF THE NEZ PERCE

Believing Howard to be far behind them, Looking Glass allowed the column to slacken its pace as he led them into the Bear Paw Mountains.

This allowed the people to regain their strength and gave the hunters time to secure food for their families. On September 29, hunters killed several buffalo, and Looking Glass ordered an early stop to the procession and insisted they would camp there until morning. A warrior named *Wottolen* protested and related that he had had a dream the night before that the soldiers would attack them at dawn. As before, Looking Glass brushed aside any concerns, and the column stopped to camp. As the Nez Perce established their camps along a protective ridge that ran the length of Snake Creek, they were unaware that a fourth army under the command of General Nelson Miles was almost upon them.

It was only on September 30 that the Nez Perce recognized that Miles and his command were within striking distance and quickly made preparations to escape from the treeless plain where they had camped the night before. They were only 30 miles from their destination—tantalizingly close. However, as the Nez Perce began to ready their horses for escape, Miles attacked. The reassurances of Looking Glass had proved to be wrong for a second time. Most of the families were not packed and ready to leave when the attack came, and the camp was again plunged into chaos.

## NELSON MILES ATTACKS
## THE FLEEING INDIANS

As during the attack at Snake Creek, Joseph ran toward the horses, while the warriors sought out their weapons and moved into offensive positions. While Miles's cavalry attacked head-on and drew the attention of the Nez Perce warriors, a second column of cavalry attacked from the side and scattered the horses Joseph had been desperately trying to move into the camp. Hundreds of the Indian horses were driven off, and the Nez Perce were left running for their lives amid the coulees and ravines of the creek. Joseph managed to seize a horse for his 12-year-old daughter, Hophoponmi, and in the chaos, shouted at her to ride for the north; he would never see her again. Joseph also managed to mount a horse, but without a weapon, he was defenseless against the soldiers. The horse he was riding was wounded, and he could feel the heat of the soldiers' bullets passing by his flesh. It seemed to him that "there were guns on every side." Joseph managed to make his way back to his lodge and there his wife Heyoon Yoyikt met him with his rifle. Thrusting it into his hands she shouted, "Here's your gun. Fight!"[27]

Moving to higher ground, Joseph left his family and took up a position among the rocks with the other warriors, including his brother, Ollokot. Despite their position among the rocks, they were not safe. As Joseph recalled, "The soldiers kept up a continuous fire. Six of my men were killed in one spot near me."[28] The accuracy of the Nez Perce warriors' guns was able to keep the soldiers from advancing, but Miles's troops established a skirmish line around the camp in order to prevent the Indians from escaping. Miles ordered another wave of attacks, one of which took his men into Joseph's camp. Joseph and his warriors repulsed the attacked, killing three of the soldiers, but losing three warriors in the process.

By the end of the day, 18 men and 3 women in Joseph's camp had been killed, and Miles was acutely aware that charging the Indians' position was futile. Instead of calling for retreat, he ordered his men to settle in for a siege. At the end of that first day's fighting, the Nez Perce had lost 22 of their people, including Ollokot. The soldiers had lost almost 60 men. As night began to settle over the battlefield, 6 Nez Perce warriors were dispatched to sneak through the soldiers' lines and make their way to Sitting Bull to request his help. The women in the meantime dug shelters into the sides of the ravines and coulees and buried the dead. As they labored, a cold wind began to blow, and soon snow drifted into the encampment.

## Negotiations with General Miles

By the morning, five inches of snow blanketed the area, and the Nez Perce were pinned down by Miles's troops. Yellow Wolf, who had fought so valiantly over the summer months, recalled, "I felt the end coming."[29] Sporadic gunfire continued through the morning, and by afternoon, Miles raised a white flag and called over that he wanted to talk to Joseph. A hurried council was held, and Looking Glass and White Bird expressed concerns that Joseph might surrender to Miles, but Joseph insisted he would only see what Miles wanted. For Nelson Miles, the drama that was playing out before him carried with it several concerns. He feared a possible Nez Perce alliance with Sitting Bull could overwhelm his position and result in a bloody massacre. At the same time, he wanted the glory of having captured Joseph and ending the war. With these thoughts racing through his mind, he awaited his meeting with the Red Napoleon.

Joseph met with Miles within the soldiers' encampment and, through the interpretative skills of a half Nez Perce, half Delaware Indian named Tom Hill, insisted that he wanted to return to the Wallowa Valley in peace. Miles asked Joseph to surrender his forces, which Joseph refused. Miles indicated the Nez Perce would be returned to Idaho, but that they needed to surrender first. Unable to reach a consensus, Joseph returned to his camp and reported to the other chiefs what had been said. A short while later, he returned to Miles's camp, and again Miles demanded the surrender of the Nez Perce. For a second time his demand was refused, but this time, Miles detained Joseph instead of allowing him to return to his people.

As a captive of the deceitful general, Joseph still held out hope for a Nez Perce victory and escape: "I knew that we were near Sitting Bull's camp in King George's land, and I thought maybe the Nez Perce who had escaped would return with assistance."[30] Through that long night, Joseph and his people waited, but no one came. While Joseph was being held in Miles's camp an impetuous army officer named Lieutenant Lovell Jerome intentionally walked into the Indian camp and was taken prisoner. By October 2, after more than a day as a captive, Joseph and Jerome were exchanged. No terms of surrender had been agreed to by Joseph, and the siege continued.

## GENERAL HOWARD ENTERS THE SCENE

By the fifth day of the siege, October 4, Howard arrived on the scene, and Miles relinquished command to him. The following day, Howard sent several Christianized Nez Perce across the lines to talk to Joseph about surrender. Howard promised that the military would take his people to Fort Keogh along the Tongue River for the winter and then return them to the Northwest in the spring. There would be no punishment for the depredations that had occurred over that long summer, but they would need to reside on the reservation.

The chiefs met in council again, and despite their desperate situation, many still opposed surrender. However, their voices were tempered by many more who longed to return to their homes and wanted to believe in the promises of the generals, including Joseph. Looking Glass warned him not to believe the word of those who had lied to them in the past. "If you surrender, you will be sorry, and in your sorrow you will feel rather to be dead,"[31] but for Joseph the choice was clear. His people were without food or shelter, and they would soon freeze to death in the cold winter snow.

As Joseph would later recall, "I could not bear to see my wounded men and women suffer any longer; we had lost enough already. General Miles had promised that we might return to our country with what stock we had left. I thought we could start again."[32]

## SURRENDER

The council decided that each chief would make his own decision, but that those who wished to continue their flight would be given as much assistance as possible by those who surrendered. Joseph revealed to his

*Brigadier General Nelson A. Miles and Buffalo Bill viewing an Indian camp near Pine Ridge Agency, South Dakota. By Grabill, January 16, 1891. National Archives.*

*Nelson A. Miles in an undated photograph. Miles led the forces that eventually trapped the Nez Perce people at Bear Paw. The promises he would make to Joseph and his people would not be kept by the government he represented. Courtesy Library of Congress, LC-DIG-ggbain-23781.*

people that he planned to surrender; too many of their people had died. Joseph's decision to abandon the flight was perhaps reinforced by what happened next. While Joseph was preparing his people for surrender, an Indian called that a rider was approaching across the plains. Many within the beleaguered Indian camp hoped that it was Sitting Bull and his warriors. Looking Glass was among those who held out this hope and rose to his feet to get a better look at the approaching rider. However, when the old chief rose to his feet to get a better look, a shot from Miles's camp rang out, and he was struck in the forehead and killed instantly. The man whom he had strained to see turned out to be one of Miles's scouts.

Looking Glass would be the last casualty in the Nez Perce War. For Joseph the flight from their home had been a costly one. His brother and closest ally was dead; his wife Springtime had been wounded; his baby girl was ill; and his eldest daughter had escaped across the plains on that first day, and he did not know whether she was alive or dead. He was painfully aware that he had been unable to protect her, just as he had been unable to protect so many of his band. He had witnessed the deaths of many of the great warriors of his people, and despite following the war chiefs along the trail that finally led them to Bear Paw, Joseph had always wanted and counseled for peace.

At two o'clock that afternoon, Joseph mounted his horse and, with five warriors accompanying him, rode to the camp of General Howard. Surrounded by soldiers, Joseph dismounted and, cradling his rifle in his arm, approached Howard and Miles. Stopping before the men who had pursued his people relentlessly for so many weeks, Joseph paused, handed over his weapon, and delivered an address that has found its way into legend. Joseph concluded with the words, "Hear me my chiefs. I am tired. My heart is sick and sad. From where the sun now stands I will fight no more forever."[33] The flight of the Nez Perce had ended, but for many, their troubles were just beginning.

## NOTES

1. Josephy, *The Nez Perce*, 490.

2. U.S. War Department, *Annual Report of the Secretary of War, Volume 1,* Letter from John Monteith to J. Q. Smith, February 9, 1877 (Washington, DC: U.S. Government Printing Office, 1877) ,115.

3. Richard W. Etulain and Glenda Riley, *Chiefs and Generals: Nine Men Who Shaped the American West* (Golden, CO: Fulcrum Publishing, 2004), 75.

4. Josephy, *The Nez Perce*, 490.

5. U.S. War Department, *Annual Report of the Secretary of War, Volume 1,* Letter from General O. O. Howard to Secretary of War, James D. Cameron, May 22, 1877, 593.

6. Ibid.

7. Joseph, *That All People May Be One People.*

8. U.S. War Department, *Annual Report, Volume 1,* Letter from General O. O. Howard to Secretary of War, James D. Cameron, May 22, 1877, 595.

9. Nerburn, *Chief Joseph*, 81.

10. Ibid.

11. Joseph, *That All People May Be One People*, 18.

12. Ibid., 19.

13. Ibid., 20.

14. Ibid., 21.

15. Ibid., 23.

16. Ibid., 25.

17. Josephy, *The Nez Perce*, 523.

18. Ibid., 524.

19. Joseph, *That All People May Be One People*, 26.

20. Josephy, *The Nez Perce*, 531.

21. Ibid., 542.

22. Joseph, *That All People May Be One People*, 28.

23. Ibid., 29.

24. Josephy, *The Nez Perce*, 599.

25. Brian Schofield, *Selling Your Father's Bones: America's 140 Year War Against the Nez Perce Tribe* (New York: Simon & Schuster, 2009), 196.

26. Nerburn, *Chief Joseph*, 175.

27. Joseph, *That All People May Be One People*, 32.

28. Ibid., 33.

29. McWhorter, *Yellow Wolf*, 212.

30. Joseph, *That All People May Be One People*, 35.

31. Nerburn, *Chief Joseph*, 266.

32. Joseph, *That All People May Be One People*, 36.

33. Josephy, *The Nez Perce*, 630.

# Chapter 5

# THE END OF NEZ PERCE INDEPENDENCE

## THE NEZ PERCE SURRENDER

Once Joseph had surrendered his weapon, he was escorted into a large tent and there remained under guard. The sight of Joseph's surrender prompted several other Indians to rise from their hiding places and to take their place with him in captivity. Slowly the process of surrender continued throughout the day and into the evening. By the ones and twos, men, women and children gave themselves up. Eventually, 87 men, 184 women, and 147 children surrendered to the military. Each trusted that the promises of the white man would be upheld and they would be allowed to return to their lands.

They were a ragged and pitiful sight. The people who came forward were not the unrepentant warriors that Miles and Howard had made them out to be, or even the proud and resplendent people who rode out of Stevensville only two months earlier. Most were half starved, many were wounded or aged. Several were unable to walk without assistance. They wore rags and struggled over the rocks because their feet had been cut on the sharp stones and they had no shoes to wear, or blankets to keep themselves warm.

*Bird's-eye view of the Nez Perce Agency, Idaho, in 1879, two years after the Nez Perce flight. It would be several more years before any members of the tribe were allowed to return home. National Archives.*

By the evening the surrender was almost complete, only a trickle more would enter into the soldier's camp. Those who had decided not to surrender were left with what weapons, ammunition, food, and supplies that could be secured. With these meager resources, those who had decided against surrender waited for darkness. As the sky turned inky black with only the sliver of a crescent moon in the sky above them, White Bird led the remaining Nez Perce out of the canyon and away from their families, their friends and their way of life. To those who remained behind in the camp of the soldiers, they like Joseph, believed in Miles and the promises he had made, and they desperately needed to rest.

## Howard's Anger at the Escaping Nez Perce

After the night had passed and the surrender was complete, Joseph walked among his people. Comforting them and providing what care he could or securing aid from the soldiers who stood guard over them. Two of the women who had surrendered were the widows of Looking Glass, without the protection of the old chief they were bereft of hope. Joseph would eventually take both as his wives. The next day, both the Nez Perce and the soldiers crowded into the battlefield and solemnly collected their dead. The soldiers dug a large pit and buried their dead in a mass grave on the top of a hill while the Nez Perce laid their people to rest in the shelters they had dug into the earth over the days the battle raged around them.

When Howard discovered that White Bird and many of the warriors had escaped, he was incensed and told Joseph that he had violated the terms of surrender. Joseph reminded him that he had not surrendered, only agreed to stop fighting, as had all who came into the soldiers' camp. White Bird and those who followed him had chosen to continue to Canada. Joseph could no more speak for White Bird than Lawyer had been able to speak for all of the Nez Perce in the treaty of 1863. Howard let the issue rest, but remained angry at both Miles for not ensuring all the Indians surrendered and Joseph for what he considered to be his duplicity.

For Howard the relief that the Nez Perce had surrendered was tempered by his concern that Sitting Bull might still decide to leave his sanctuary in Canada and again wage war in America. A half-hearted search party was sent out to look for White Bird and his band, and while a few wounded Indians were found and returned, the Nez Perce had made good their escape. Since the crisis that had riveted the attention of the nation for the summer was now concluded, Howard made ready to leave the Bear Paw Mountains and return to his command in the Columbia Plateau. Miles would attend to the transport of Joseph's band to Fort Keogh and their incarceration through the winter. The trip would take them back over much of the terrain they had only recently crossed.

### Preparations for the Nez Perce Winter Incarceration

To manage the logistics of the move, Miles and Joseph were often seen walking and talking together; at their side was Arthur Chapman, the settler who had started the fight at White Bird Canyon and who was now serving as an interpreter for the military. Joseph was content to have his people winter in the buffalo country, but he asked that the rifles be returned to his men. Only with their weapons would his people be able to hunt and feed themselves. Miles firmly and repeatedly refused his request.

The second day after Chief Joseph had relinquished his gun to Nelson Miles, the soldiers and their captives began their long journey to their winter quarters. While Joseph trusted the word of Nelson Miles and his terms to end the war, these were not terms agreed to by the U.S. government, and soon Joseph and his people would realize their surrender had condemned them to a fate many would have considered worse than fighting to the death in the Bear Paw Mountains.

## THE GOVERNMENT RENEGES ON ITS PROMISES

Since June the federal government had endured jibs and criticism about what many called the Nez Perce War. The competence of the army's commanders from the field level all the way up to the commander of the army, William Tecumseh Sherman, was questioned. No one was spared in the criticism and the blame for the deaths of the settlers was laid at the feet of the government and their toleration of a group of people many Americans considered "savages." In the public mind, the military had been bested time and again by a group who many Americans held in contempt and who they considered to be inferior. That the Nez Perce Indians had proven themselves to be a force to be contended with chipped at the fragile ego of the American psyche. In 1876 Sitting Bull came to personify the slaughter of Custer at the Little Big Horn, and while there was not the stunning loss of life in comparison with the Nez Perce War, Joseph nonetheless came to be regarded as the greatest warrior of the Nez Perce tribe, at least by white Americans.

It was that great warrior, who now solemnly rode next to Miles at the head of the procession that left the Bear Paw Mountains. The battle had been devastating on several levels to the Nez Perce; more than two dozen members of the tribe had died during the fighting while many more had been wounded and would later die from their wounds. Families had been divided, not just by death, but also by those who chose to cross into Canada. Even Joseph could feel the pain of remorse as his daughter had been one of those to escape, and as the camp chief, it was his responsibility to tend to the almost 500 people who were now in the hands of people they had considered their enemies. As the press continued to rail against the incompetence of the military, the wounded feelings of the military became secondary to a larger issue for the Nez Perce.

The Wallowa Valley was a prime location for agriculture and white settlers wanted the land to build farms; the sale of the land would raise revenue for the government and votes for its politicians. If the land were to be given back to the Indians, the public outcry would be considerable. A small chorus of criticism had forced Ulysses Grant to revoke an executive order that had created the Nez Perce reservation in 1875, a mere two years after it had been issued. Now that more people lived in the region, the criticism would be greater. There was also the concern that if the government allowed the Indians to return to the Wallowa Valley, this would send the wrong message to the other Indian tribes in the nation. A message that rebellion against the government would eventually get them what they wanted.

## FORT KEOGH

The wounded pride of the U.S. military, however, would prove to be the immediate problem that Joseph and his people had to face. Both Howard and Miles had made promises to Joseph in order to secure his surrender, promises that the military had no intention of keeping. The recent criticism leveled by the press and the political realities of conditions in the Pacific Northwest had resulted in an ardent desire by high ranking members of the military to get out of what many called the "Indian business." There would be little attempt to try to sway the government to honor the promises made in the field.

As they journeyed toward Fort Keogh, Joseph took the time to relate the Nez Perce version of the events that had led to their flight to Nelson Miles. His words were translated by Arthur Chapman who assumed a position between the two men and dutifully translated Joseph's words. For almost two weeks they traveled until they came to the confluence of the Tongue and Yellowstone rivers, and there saw Fort Keogh for the first time. According to the promises of Howard and Miles, this would be their winter quarters and in the spring the tribe would return to their homelands.

With the weather beginning to cool considerably, Joseph and his people quickly began to establish a camp just outside the fort in a grove of trees that would afford them some protection from the icy wind and snow that would blanket the plains in the coming months. However, as they labored, William Sherman sent an order to Miles to relocate his charges to Fort Abraham Lincoln in the Dakota Territory, a distance of more than 300 miles. The reason for the move was simple economics, the town of Bismarck, which was near the fort, was the end of the line for the railroad and supplying food and other necessities to the hundreds of Indians would be cheaper. From there the Indians would be moved to some other location, probably Indian Country in what is now Oklahoma.

## Miles Informs Joseph of the Government's Decision

Nelson Miles protested the movement of the Nez Perce to the new location. Five of the Nez Perce had died on the journey from Bear Paw to Fort Keogh, and his agreement with Joseph at Bear Paw was that the Nez Perce would return to Idaho. Miles's protests fell on deaf ears. The Indians had been in active rebellion against the government and in Sherman's mind they had forfeited all of their rights. No agreements would be honored, the Indians would do as they were told. Unhappily, Miles prepared Joseph for what lay ahead and insisted, "You must not blame me. I have endeavored to keep my word, but the chief who is over me has given the order, and I must obey it or resign. That would do you no good. Some other officer would carry out the order."[1]

Despite his disappointment, Joseph did not blame Nelson Miles and believed that "Miles would have kept his word if he could have done so."[2] With a heavy heart, he informed his people of the government's decision to relocate them to the Dakota Territory. In disbelief and sorrow, the Nez Perce halted their activities and began to break down their camp. As the people began to struggle to overcome the injustice being done to them, concerns began to filter to the surface of their consciousness. Would the government allow them to return to their homes after all, and if not, where would they go?

## SEPARATION OF THE NEZ PERCE AND THE LOSS OF THE HERDS

The order to move the Nez Perce came at an inopportune time, the weather was beginning to change, ice was already forming in the river ways and travel would be difficult. To compound this, the Nez Perce were weary from months of exhausting travel and hardship; a cold and difficult journey would likely result in further tragedy. Miles recognized that more of the Nez Perce would die before they reached their destination, so 14 flat-bottomed boats were secured for the wounded, the elderly, and the very young to travel on. The rest of the Nez Perce would travel overland, riding on their own horses or in wagons. Since time was important, most of the Nez Perce herds would be left behind, more than 1,100 horses.

Joseph protested the division of his people and the loss of their property. To separate would mean the most vulnerable members of his band would be without his protection, and their horses represented most of their wealth and security. Without their horses they would be unable to hunt and support their families. Joseph's repeated protests however, did not alter the outcome; the Nez Perce were the captives of the government and would be forced to comply with the orders they had received.

## TRAGEDY ON THE RIVER

Perhaps to quiet Joseph's concerns, Miles announced he would travel part of the way on one of the rafts. His presence would secure the protection that Joseph could not offer to his people. On October 31, 1877, the last of the Nez Perce were loaded onto wagons for the journey to Fort Abraham Lincoln and headed off on a slow march toward the southeast. They would rejoin their families farther down the river. The rest clamored onto the boats and prepared to make the dangerous journey on the river. As the boats struggled against the swollen rivers and the ice that choked the waters, tragedy struck. One of the boats was overwhelmed in rough current and threw all of its riders into the icy water. Despite efforts to save them, all on board were lost.

Two days later, Miles lost his taste for river travel, and when his boat overtook the land party, he abandoned it and continued the rest of the journey on horseback. As the boats continued along the river, several more accidents occurred and many more Nez Perce were lost. The boatmen struggled to control their boats, but the rapidly deteriorating weather conditions caused the water to churn; the rough waters when coupled with the shallow drafts of the boats made the task of controlling the crafts difficult and in some cases, impossible. Almost two weeks after leaving Fort Keogh, the Nez Perce began to arrive at Fort Buford. Here the land and rivers parties would meet and rest a few days before beginning the final leg of their journey to Fort Lincoln. By the time the first boats landed near Fort Buford, it was already mid-November; the last of the overland group arrived at Fort Abraham Lincoln two days later. Snow was already falling, and the temperatures at night were bitterly cold. Despite the hardships they had endured over the previous two weeks, the Nez Perce were still 10 days away from their final destination, the Dakota Territory.

## BISMARCK, NORTH DAKOTA

The arrival of the Nez Perce had been widely anticipated by the people of the bustling city of Bismarck in the Dakota Territory. As Bismarck was one of the fastest growing cities in the West, the residents of the town were in a unique position to welcome the Red Napoleon and his captor into their midst. They did so in a style that must have warmed the hearts of the Nez Perce. As the Indians, led by Chief Joseph on horseback, reached the crest of the hill overlooking the town they saw the streets lined with the citizens and soldiers. A moment later a military band broke into "The Star Spangled Banner," and the crowd surged forward. Women and children held out dishes of food to the exhausted tribe. Surprised, but pleased, the Nez Perce accepted the offerings as one of the few kindnesses shown them for many long months. After their reception the tribe was ushered into an area along the river where they would camp for the winter.

That evening the town gave a banquet in honor of Nelson Miles and while Nelson reveled in the attention, he also made a point to repeat the things that Joseph had told him following his capture. All the abuses the Indians had endured at the hand of the government and corrupt Indian agents, and even the humane way the Nez Perce fought the war. They did not scalp their victims as the Sioux had the year before when they destroyed Custer's troops at the Little Big Horn, instead they had been known to offer assistance and comfort to soldiers who had been wounded. The story Nelson Miles related was one of a people who had struggled and yet still sought peace despite the abuses they had endured. When he had finished the town leaders decided a second banquet was in order, this one would be for Joseph.

## Joseph and Miles Speak Publically about the War

Miles's careful rendition of the Indian struggle had piqued the curiosity of several of the men who were at the banquet that evening. Together they approached Miles and requested the opportunity to speak with Joseph. To accommodate their request and to frame the actions of the military and the Nez Perce in the best light possible the following day Joseph and Miles met a group of reporters. There Joseph recalled again the abuses endured by his people and repeated his request to return to his homeland.

Miles also spoke to the reporters, but his statements and the press releases he had sent ahead of his arrival would create a rivalry between himself and Oliver Howard; he marginalized Howard's efforts to capture the Nez Perce and showcased his own. Howard's straggling campaign and failure to capture the Nez Perce after many months ignored the reality that the Nez Perce had also fought Miles to a standstill and it was only the arrival of Howard that had given the military the tactical advantage over the Indians. Had the Sioux arrived as many had feared, the outcome of a battle between the Indians and the soldiers would have been anyone's guess.

Miles also announced that he had been recalled to the East where he was to make a full report to his superiors of the events of the previous months. Miles's news concerned Joseph. Miles had made promises to the tribe, and without him to ensure those promises would be kept the Nez Perce would suffer. Joseph's concerns were not unfounded but he could do little; he could not order Miles to remain with his people, and only hoped that the words of the government would prove to be true. His hopes would be in vain. Miles reassured Joseph that their agreements would be honored and left later that evening without telling the Nez Perce chief the rest of the information he had received after their surrender. The Nez Perce stay at Bismarck would be brief, orders had already been passed down from Washington for the tribe to be transported to Fort Leavenworth by train and then to Indian Country the following year.

## Joseph Is Honored by the People of Bismarck

The following day, Joseph and many of his people were allowed to shop in the town. Because the Indians had been forced to abandon most of their possessions over the preceding months this was good news. The town's newspaper reported that Joseph made several purchases and described his movements about the town in noble, almost regal terms. That evening Joseph was invited to the banquet that would be held in his honor, and he happily accepted. A few hours later he arrived at the Sheridan House Hotel with Husishusis Kute, Yellow Bull, and several other Nez Perce leaders. After a filling dinner, the Nez Perce and white leaders gave a series of speeches, expressing their gratitude and mutual wish for peace. While the Nez Perce were buoyed by the experience, their happiness would not last.

That evening after the festivities had ended, Arthur Chapman advised Joseph that his people would be forced to continue on to Fort Leavenworth in Kansas. Joseph protested the move, the people of Bismarck had welcomed his people and they were preparing their camp for the winter. However, his protests fell on deaf ears. As Joseph now knew, the rights of the Nez Perce had been jettisoned the moment of their surrender at Bear Paw.

On November 23, the Nez Perce were loaded onto a train that would take them away from Bismarck. They were unable to take their remaining horses with them. Now without weapons or horses the Nez Perce were truly at the mercy of the government. For the next four days the band traveled to the south. At many stops along the route, throngs of people would meet the train. They cheered when Joseph stepped into view and pressed him to speak or gave him gifts. Joseph politely complied with many of their requests. He was beginning to understand the size and strength of the nation that now had his people in its power. He also began to understand that his presence and his words were sought after, and important to them. His understanding of these things would serve his people well in the future.

## FORT LEAVENWORTH, KANSAS

At Fort Leavenworth, the Indians were sent to live in canvas tepees that had been arranged along the river. The terrain around them was flat and the ground was soft with the moisture that spread out from the river. It bore no resemblance to their home more than 1,500 miles away in the Wallowa Valley. As Joseph later recalled, "At Leavenworth we were placed on a low river bottom with no water except river water to drink and cook with. We had always lived in a healthy country where the mountains were high and the water was cold and clear. Many of our people sickened and died, and we buried them in this strange land."[3]

The townspeople were there to greet the train, but not as the residents of Bismarck had, with food and celebration. Instead they crowded around him and when they tried to speak to Joseph, he was unable to understand them. Disappointed, they left. However, as time passed many would return over and over again to the Indian encampment to seek him out. He granted several interviews to reporters about the recent war, and he also reminded the people of the United States that their general had promised they could return to their home in the Wallowa Valley. Soon so many people came, as many as 5,000 in a single day, that the commander of Fort Leavenworth limited outside visitation to twice a week.

Tirelessly, Joseph spoke about his people and their desire to return home. He sent a letter to William Sherman asking that the promises of Nelson Miles and Oliver Howard be honored. However, Sherman was resolute in his denial of their rights; the public's criticism of how the Nez Perce War had been fought reflected badly on him. He did not want to involve the military any further than it had to be in the affairs of the Nez Perce people. Joseph's people would remain where he had placed them until the military was able to discharge its obligation and the Nez Perce had been removed to Indian Country.

## Deteriorating Conditions at Fort Leavenworth

By the spring of 1878, the conditions at the Fort Leavenworth Indian encampment deteriorated dramatically. As the weather warmed, the sewage from the town began to seep into the Nez Perce village. The Indians quickly fell ill and by summer almost half were ill and unable to care for themselves. Joseph's own infant daughter who had survived the rigors of their flight was ailing. To add to their misery the temperature in the area steadily climbed well into the 90s, and the resulting humidity made even routine daily tasks all the more difficult.

## BAIRD'S COMMISSION

While the Nez Perce suffered from one of the hottest summers in Kansas history, agents for the U.S. government were in Canada where they encouraged White Bird and the other Nez Perce who had escaped the military at Bear Paw to surrender. The commission, led by Lieutenant George Baird, had been intended to deflect some of the criticism that still targeted the government's treatment of the Nez Perce. If the Nez Perce in Canada would voluntarily join their kin in captivity it would indicate to the American population that much of the criticism was unfounded. To convince White Bird, three of Joseph's people were enlisted to accompany the commissioners, Yellow Bull, Husishusis Kute, and *Estoweaz*.

At a meeting on July 1 and 2, Baird promised White Bird that his people would be reunited with Joseph's band and they "would be treated just as well and have the same protection as Joseph and his people."[4] When time came for the Nez Perce to speak, they expressed Joseph's concern that they would not be allowed to return home unless the Nez Perce under White Bird joined them, but also undoubtedly advised their brothers of the conditions they had endured over the past several months. White Bird did not consent to the wholesale return of his people to the south, but several would independently make the decision to return into the United States in the coming years. Several of those who did were taken to live in Indian Territory with Joseph and the rest of the captured Nez Perce; the treatment they received there only further accentuated their mistrust of the government.

## The Move to Baxter Springs

When the negotiations with White Bird failed to bear fruit, the government began to make arrangements to move Joseph and his people to Indian Country. Their strength and health sapped by the heat, the Nez Perce finally began their journey on July 19. Sick, weak, and desperate to leave Fort Leavenworth, they were loaded onto a train that would take them, not to their mountain homes, but to the Quapaw Agency near Baxter Springs in Indian Territory, some 150 miles farther to the south. In the two-day journey, more of their people, including Joseph's wife, fell ill and three more died. By the time the band arrived at Baxter Springs, they could do little more than lie on the ground and rest.

At the Quapaw Agency, the Nez Perce were transferred from the Department of the Army to the Department of the Interior and placed under the control of an Indian agent named Hiram Jones. By the time Joseph and his people had arrived, Jones had a well-established reputation as a corrupt and vicious man. The Quapaw agency already had almost 1,400 Indian residents from several tribes, primarily from the East. Only the Modoc Indians were from the West and they would be expected to share their two and a half mile square allotment with the new arrivals. Resentful of the imposition, the Modoc helped to transport the weakened Nez Perce the following day to their reserve, but left them alone in a field without access to their belongings, most of which would eventually be stolen from them.

Over the next several weeks, the Nez Perce clung to life. Without the means of survival such as food, clean water and proper shelters, and overwhelmed by the dry oppressive heat, they continued to sicken and die at an alarming rate. Among those who would die during that awful summer was an orphaned boy that Joseph had adopted after Bear Paw. To make matters worse, within a month of their arrival at the Quapaw Agency, Joseph was formally advised that his people would not be allowed to return to their mountain homes, the land had already been taken over by settlers. Eventually, better land was secured for the Nez Perce within the Quapaw agency, but despite its beauty it still was not home. After months of struggle and enduring the sad task of watching his people suffer Joseph soon would become too depressed to care.

## ARTHUR CHAPMAN'S CHANGE OF HEART

Joseph was unable to shake the depression that settled over him and his people. They would find that in their darkest moment, one of their former enemies would soon become one of their greatest champions, Arthur Chapman. Chapman had started on the campaign trail with the military against the Nez Perce; he had foolishly led several men to their deaths at the Battle of White Bird Canyon, and since that time, he had served as an interpreter for the government and the Nez Perce people. He had been the one who translated the words of Generals Miles and Howard and of all the commanders and townsmen who had pressed Joseph for statements. During the hot days of the summer of 1878, he too had fallen ill and had suffered with them.

In the months he spent with Joseph and his people, Chapman's attitude began to change. After a month of living in squalor and victimized by the corruption of Agent Jones, Chapman decided he had had enough. At the end of August 1878, he began writing a series of letters to newspapers across the country championing the Nez Perce cause and complaining about their treatment at the hand of the government and its agent. Chapman raised such a ruckus that eventually Commissioner of Indian Affairs Ezra Hayt became involved.

Hayt attempted to assign the Nez Perce to better lands and even accompanied Joseph on a tour of lands in Indian Country. However, on their journey, Joseph made it clear that he would move to the new lands, but that they were not to be the permanent home of the Nez Perce. They still wanted to return to the land of their ancestors. No concession on

Hayt's part was made, but Joseph continued to insist the government must honor its word. Unfortunately for the Nez Perce, until they moved the following spring, they would still be under the control of Hiram Jones.

## HIRAM JONES STRIKES BACK

Jones was eager to repair his tattered reputation. As an agent for the government he had been placed in a position that allowed him to enrich himself and his family by misappropriating funds that had been sent for the benefit of the Indians in his care. To lose his position because of growing public sympathy toward the Nez Perce would close that spigot of wealth, and Jones resolved to counter Chapman's assertions. To do so he would need to silence Joseph as much as possible and marginalize Chapman's influence over the band. That autumn Joseph decided that he would also use the power of his words to convince Washington to allow his people to end their suffering and return home. He requested permission to travel to Washington, D.C., but Jones refused to allow him to travel off the reserve. Undaunted, he and the other Nez Perce collected money and sent Chapman in their stead.

While Chapman was away, Jones used the opportunity to undermine the authority of Joseph and Chapman by inviting three treaty Nez Perce to come to the agency and assist with the management of the band. These three Christianized Nez Perce—James Reuben, William and Archie Lawyer—succeeded in dividing the loyalties of the bands leaders. Husishusis Kute, the Palouse chief whose people had suffered alongside Joseph's, began to see merit in the arguments of Christianization and assimilation.

While Jones's intent had been to reduce Joseph's influence over his people and silence the complaints against him, his plan only partially succeeded. The three Christianized Nez Perce began to gain authority among Joseph's exiled people; however, the seriousness of the complaints against Jones eventually resulted in his removal as agent in the late spring of 1878. While Jones could no longer abuse Joseph's people, the divisions he had helped sow within the tribe were already beginning to solidify. Joseph realized that he would need to redouble his efforts to go to Washington to speak for his people, and with the assistance of former commissioner of Indian Affairs A. B. Meacham, he was finally given permission to travel away from the Quapaw Agency to Washington in January 1879.

Joseph's journey to Washington with Chapman and Yellow Bull caused a stir among the people they encountered. Joseph adeptly used the attention to pound out the message of his people: the Nez Perce people wanted to return home. At a presentation at Lincoln Hall in Washington, D.C., Joseph condemned any government that would not keep its word and steal from a captured people: "I have heard talk and talk, but nothing is done."[5] Eventually, Joseph would meet with President Rutherford B. Hayes and Secretary of the Interior Carl Schurz. Despite the high hopes Joseph had following their meeting, it seemed as if nothing would happen. However, the story of the Nez Perce had taken on a life of its own. In April, the *North American Review,* a popular magazine at the time, published a transcript of Joseph's speech at Lincoln Hall. As more Americans became aware of the duplicity of the government and the plight of the Indians, voices rose up to demand something be done. Unfortunately, more time would pass before the government decided to act.

## THE OAKLAND RESERVE

By June 1879, the Nez Perce were moved again, this time to the Oakland Reserve, 180 miles farther inside Indian Territory. These were the lands that Joseph had chosen during his meeting with Ezra Hayt the year before. However, when he chose the land the summer's heat had been waning and there were good pastures for the Nez Perce horses and water in a stream. Now things looked considerably different.

The new Indian agent, J. M. Haworth, proved to be considerably more competent and honest than his predecessor. He purchased wagons, horses, and extra rations for the Indians to help ease their journey. Despite his consideration, the still weak Indians struggled in the mounting heat to move to their new home. As they traveled, Joseph now aware of the power of public opinion, stopped in the newspaper offices of the towns they passed and again recounted the story of the Nez Perce and of their desire to return home. Joseph's persistence ensured that his words and the desires of his people would not be forgotten. His efforts to return them to the cool valleys of the mountains took on a greater sense of urgency when they reached their destination.

The land bore little resemblance to the land that Joseph had seen the year before. The summer's oppressive heat had dried the grass and reduced the river to a trickle by the time they arrived. The heat and the desolation of the place they would be forced to call home was compounded by further illness within the Nez Perce camp. By the summer of 1879, of the 418 men, women, and children who had followed Joseph into captivity, now only 370 survived. There were few resources for them to draw from, and conditions again became dire.

Through the hot summer of 1879 and into the next year, the Nez Perce were shown how to farm. This became the only way they were able to store enough food to sustain their livestock and feed through the harsh winters that characterized the territory. Farming was offensive to the Nez Perce, many of whom believed the plow raking across the land caused scars and displayed a lack of respect for the earth. Despite their objections, however, by the following year, even Joseph and Yellow Bull had begun to plant crops to enable their families to survive. During this time the reserve was visited by several representatives from the government and churches who were sympathetic to the Nez Perce cause. To all of them Joseph pleaded that his people be allowed to abandon the place they now called *Eekish Pah* or "the hot place" and return to their mountains.

## The Rise of James Reuben

By 1881 Joseph's authority among his people was being supplanted by James Reuben. As a Christianized Indian, James Reuben hoped to achieve several things during his time in Indian Country, the first of which was to convert the Nez Perce to Christianity, then to return them to the Lapwai Reservation in Idaho and there to teach the people to live in accordance with white ways. Regard for James Reuben grew in the surrounding white communities because he had assimilated to white ways. This allowed him to better use the resources of the surrounding communities to address the needs of his people. It was at this time that Joseph silenced his own voice in the hope that another's would be able to bring his people home.

Joseph stood passively by as James Reuben insisted the Nez Perce must farm and adopt white ways in order to survive. When James Reuben's words proved to be true and conditions improved somewhat, Joseph supported his efforts. Joseph's willingness to set aside his own ego and allow another to lead his people during their exile in Indian Country perhaps speaks more about the depth of his devotion to his people than any other action. He continued to practice the old ways as before, but acknowledged the new as well.

To survive the Nez Perce were forced to go against their traditions and to farm or to take menial jobs in the nearby town of Arkansas City. All around them death hung like a pall in the air, the cold biting winds of winter gave way to the excruciating heat of the summer, and as the seasons changed they took with them more of the Nez Perce people. Joseph's own baby daughter, the one who had been born in the tumult of their escape in 1877 also withered and died in the oppressive heat. It appeared to Joseph, and to many of his people that their Creator had forgotten them.

To many the God of the white man was their only option. Even Joseph began to listen to the words of James Reuben and at one point wrote a letter to Howard advising him that he intended to become a Christian and asking for his assistance in returning his people to their lands, as Howard had promised all those years ago. Howard's response was to deny the promise and to encourage his conversion. With Joseph's voice dimmed, James Reuben's influence among the refugees increased, especially after the conversion of Husishusis Kute. To increase the assimilation of the Indians, Reuben started a school on the agency and by the end of the first year, 38 Nez Perce were attending classes.

## Assistance from the Presbyterian Church

By the end of October 1880, Reuben petitioned the Presbyterian leaders in Arkansas City to help establish a church at the Oakland agency. To prove the sincerity of the Indians, he invited the church elders to visit. One hundred and twenty-five Nez Perce appeared for a short religious program, and 59 asked for baptism. Joseph attended the ceremony but remained outside. The Presbyterian elders enthusiastically approved the church and the first week of November the cornerstone for the new church was laid. At the ceremony, more than 200 Nez Perce appeared, including Joseph. With the foundation of a church, Joseph and his people had a new ally in their desire to return home.

The Presbyterian Church began pressing the government to allow the Indians to move to the Lapwai Reservation. Despite continued opposition from those who lived in the western states, in 1883 they were successful in forcing the government to allow 33 Nez Perce Christians to return to the Columbia Plateau and settle on the reservation. As the authority of the Christians increased on the reservation, Joseph continued to remain in the shadows; he did not interfere with the Christianized Indians or their ministers.

When one minister came to report on whether the church should promote the removal of the rest of the Nez Perce, Joseph encouraged him to relate all he had seen to the nation's leaders in Washington and to ask them to have pity on his people but did nothing else. Despite his missive to Howard and his passive support of the Christian church, Joseph did not convert to Christianity but instead continued to follow the Dreamer religion. He also continued to represent the interests of his people against settlers who attempted to defraud them or steal what little they had, but he did so with a respectful eye toward the Christians who were working among his people. He continued, in short, to be what he had always been, the leader and protector of his people in whatever way he could be.

## The Campaign to Return the Nez Perce

Despite the success in relocating some of the Christianized Nez Perce, the rest of Joseph's people would continue to languish on the desolate prairie of the Oakland reserve for another two years. However, the Presbyterians had not forgotten the plight of the Nez Perce and a campaign to force the government to relocate all the Nez Perce continued through 1884. Their efforts were aided by Nelson Miles, who had assumed command of the Department of the Columbia in 1881, and who was also pushing for the government to honor its commitment and return the Indians to their homelands.

By July 1884, Congress finally relented and authorized the return of the Nez Perce. The only issue to be ironed out was where would they go? The Lapwai Reservation was a Christian enclave and while the

Christianized Indians could settle there, Joseph and the other traditional Indians would not be welcome. Nor could Joseph and his band return to the Wallowa Valley, because the area had been given over entirely to white settlement. In the end Joseph and his people decided they would divide: the Christianized Nez Perce would live on the Lapwai Reservation and the traditional Nez Perce would move to the Colville Reservation some 200 miles to the north in the state of Washington.

## The Return Home

Finally, on May 21, 1885, the Nez Perce were allowed to begin their long journey home. They left behind the graves of more than 100 of their people at the Oakland agency and countless others on the treacherous trails and canyons they had traversed since their odyssey began seven years earlier. As before they were forced to sell or abandon much of their property, and as a final injustice the Nez Perce were compelled to formally relinquish title to their lands in Indian Country to a government agent. Joseph and the other chiefs signed because they had no choice. As the train approached their homeland, the Nez Perce were individually forced to make a decision, to settle on the Lapwai or the Colville reservations. In the end, 118 chose Lapwai Reservation, and 150 followed Joseph to the Colville Reservation and into exile.

# THE COLVILLE RESERVATION

The transition into a life on the Colville Reservation was not an easy one. The area, while similar in terrain to the Wallowa Valley, was shared by several different tribes, and most were unhappy they were now required to share their land with another group. In addition, the agent was hostile to Joseph and his people because of the damage that had been done during the Nez Perce War. He did little to accommodate the Nez Perce unless forced to by his superiors. The hope that the Nez Perce might return to their traditional lands was all but crushed in 1887 when the Dawes Severalty Act was passed.

The Dawes Act was the government's attempt to get out of the "Indian business." Under its provisions, the reservations that belonged to the Indians would be divided into individual allotments and whatever lands remained would be opened up for sale to the public. Joseph was allotted land on the Lapwai Reservation, but refused to accept it as he feared this would negate his claim to the Wallowa Valley. Instead of agreeing to the allotment of the lands of his people Joseph went to the courts to press the government for the return of their lands and to compensate them for all they had lost over the years. To press his case he made several more trips to the East, but in each instance he was ignored.

## JOSEPH'S CONTINUED WORK FOR HIS PEOPLE

As the nation continued to expand, the ways of the West faded into a romanticized past. Joseph's claims to land that had long been occupied by white settlers were not taken seriously, although he continued to push forward his claim. However, as the nation plunged toward the modernity of the 20th century many longed for the simpler time of the old West. To those seeking the nostalgia of the past, Joseph often found himself used as window dressing for events that did little to advance his cause. He spoke at the dedication of Grant's Tomb in 1897 and participated in Wild Bill Cody's Wild West Show in 1903. All to little avail.

Undaunted, Joseph continued to press for the return of the lands of his ancestors. In the summer of 1900, Joseph was allowed to return to the Wallowa Valley for the first time since his flight in 1877. He visited the graves of his parents and wept openly over all he had lost in the previous 23 years. Later on he appeared before the town of Enterprise in the Wallowa Valley to ask the residents there for land in the Imnaha Valley. The crowd refused his request outright. Joseph still hoped that a special agent for the Indian Commissioner, a man named James McLaughlin would inspect the area and agree that Joseph and his people could return home. When McLaughlin filed his report, he showed no sympathy for Joseph's position and the commission accepted his recommendation that Joseph remain on the Colville Reservation.

### Joseph's Final Days

On the Colville Reservation as a landless sojourner, Joseph continued to defiantly and resolutely insist upon leading his life in accordance with the traditions of his people. When the government decided to send the Nez Perce children to a school that was off the Colville Reservation, Joseph refused to send them. Instead he and his people held to their traditions and insisted they alone had the right to raise their children in accordance with the ways of their ancestors. Joseph remained the leader of the Wallowa band of Nez Perce throughout his life. True to the promise he made to his father so many years before he cared and protected his people as best he could from anything that threatened them. However, as the 20th century dawned, Joseph's life was nearing its end.

In 1903 gold was discovered on the Colville Reservation and half the land was given over to mining. Joseph made one final trip that year to the East to speak with the new president, Theodore Roosevelt, and ask again whether his people might return to their home in the Wallowa Valley. While their meeting was cordial, nothing came of it. Roosevelt, while sympathetic to the plight of the Indians and the romance of the Old West, believed in progress and returning the land to the Nez Perce would hinder that progress.

On his journey home, Joseph stopped at the Carlisle School in Pennsylvania to commemorate the anniversary of the school's founding. There he met up with his old nemesis, Oliver Howard, and there he repeated his commitment to live in peace with all people. No doubt he was painfully aware that that commitment to peace had cost he and his people dearly. As Joseph entered the open fields of the Colville Reservation he was a man worn down by the demands of leadership. As the year progressed he became frailer and remained for long hours by himself staring listlessly into space and refusing to speak.

In the 64 years of his life, Joseph had fathered nine children; all would precede him in death, as well as the countless orphans he brought into his home. He married four times, but by the time of his death in 1904, only two of his wives remained, the two widows of Looking Glass. He had seen his people welcome and then be betrayed by the same white men who came onto their lands, and despite public misperceptions, he was not the man of war most thought him to be; instead he was a man of peace. He had suffered unjustly at the hands of a government because of the arrogance and greed of its people, and yet he remained resolutely devoted to his people and to the ideal of peace. For Joseph the struggles that he had been forced to endure would end on September 21, 1904. After sitting quietly for some time he called his wife to him and asked her to retrieve his headdress, telling her, "I wish to die as a chief." While she was gone, Joseph died.[6]

# CONCLUSION

For many, the story of Joseph and the Nez Perce is one of sorrow and loss, painful to recite and to imagine. The unnecessary and seemingly unending suffering of a group of people simply because of the greed and contempt of another is a tragedy at any time and among any nation. However, the Nez Perce, true to the gifts given to them by the Creator rose above the hardships imposed upon them, and despite not being allowed to occupy the Wallowa Valley as their ancestors had for generations before them, they have come home.

They have survived as a people, and they have flourished. Many would be angry at Joseph for his pacifism and willingness to believe in the word of the white man, especially when the evidence against his white captors mounted. How could he have been so foolish to have believed, when all others did not? The answer can be found in who and what Joseph was. He had been raised to be a guardian of his people, to care for their needs and to protect them in times of trouble. While war chiefs led charges against their enemies, Joseph ensured their people would live on long past the hour of battle. He tended the young and the aged, the sick, and the wounded. He welcomed the children into the world he knew, and buried those who had exhausted their time on earth. Joseph was truly a man of his people. He embodied their values, their hopes, and their culture.

When circumstances robbed him of all he held dear, he responded resolutely and in the manner of his people, with quiet, restrained dignity. Despite the insults hurled at him, and the lies told to him, Joseph refused to allow his humanity and his dignity to be stripped away. More uniquely was that he continued to view even those who had wronged him through a rare lens of humanity and forgiveness. In doing so, he reminded them of their humanity and their obligation to their fellow man. For these reasons, In-mut-too-yah-lat-lat of the Wellamotkin band of the Nez Perce is and will remain one of the great chiefs of the Nez Perce people and one of the great men of all time.

## NOTES

1. Joseph, *That All People May Be One People*, 37.

2. Ibid.

3. Ibid., 38.

4. Jerome Greene and Alvin Josephy, Jr., *Nez Perce Summer, 1877: The U.S. Army and the Nee-Me-Poo Crisis* (Helena, MT: Montana Historical Society, 2001), 344.

5. Joseph, *That All People May Be One People*, 41.

6. Nerburn, *Chief Joseph*, 396.

# IMPORTANT PEOPLE AND PLACES IN THE LIFE OF CHIEF JOSEPH

**Abernathy, George**   Provisional governor of the Oregon Territory 1845–1849.

*Ah-cum-kin-i-ma-me-hut*   Nez Perce Creator.

*Aihits Palojami*   (Fair Land) Wife of Ollokot. Killed at the Battle of Big Hole.

*Allalimya Takanin*   (Looking Glass) Chief of the Nez Perce. Led the Nez Perce through most of the Nez Perce War. Killed at the Battle of Bear Paw Mountain.

*Apash Wyakaikt*   (Flint Necklace) Chief who met Lewis and Clark in 1805. Grandfather of Looking Glass who would lead the Nez Perce into exile in 1877.

**Baird, George**   Lieutenant, U.S. Army. Negotiated for the return of White Bird to the United States after the end of the Nez Perce War.

**Barstow, A. C.**   Peace commissioner during the summer of 1876.

**Beckroge, Henry**   Settler in the Wallowa Valley. Killed by *Wahkitits* at the outset of the Nez Perce War.

**Benedict, Samuel**    Settler in the Wallowa Valley. Wounded by *Wahkitits* at the outset of the Nez Perce War.

**Black Hair**    Nez Perce warrior. His vision of Howard's horses on the trail led the Nez Perce to raid the herds of the military.

**Bland, Robert**    Settler in the Wallowa Valley. Killed by *Wahkitits* at the outset of the Nez Perce War.

**Blue Cloak**    Nez Perce chief and early convert to Christianity.

**Boyle, William**    Lieutenant, U.S. Army. Assigned to Fort Walla Walla.

**Brouillet, Father John Baptiste**    Catholic missionary in the Willamette Valley at the time of the Whitman Massacre.

**Canby, Edward**    General, U.S. Army. Killed during the Modoc War in 1872.

**Canfield, William**    Survivor of the Whitman Massacre who warned Eliza Spalding of the trouble and helped to protect her.

**Chapman, Arthur**    Settler who started the fighting at White Bird Canyon and later would prove to be an ally of the Nez Perce.

**Cornoyer, Major**    Indian agent on the Umatilla Reservation in 1877.

**Cowen, Mrs. George**    Held captive in Yellowstone Park by the Nez Perce.

**Custer, George Armstrong**    General, U.S. Army. Died June 1876 at the Battle of Little Big Horn.

*Dakoopin*    Crippled Nez Perce Indian; killed by Richard Devine when he begged for food.

**Delano, Columbus**    Secretary of the Interior (1870–1875).

**Devine, Richard**    Settler in the Wallowa Valley. Killed by *Wahkitits* at the outset of the Nez Perce War.

**Disoway, Gabriel**    Pushed for Methodist missionaries to go to Nez Perce country in 1836.

*Eekish Pah*    (the hot place) Name given to the land the Nez Perce occupied in Indian Country during their captivity from 1877 to 1885.

**Elfers, Henry**    Settler in the Wallowa Valley. Killed by *Wahkitits* at the outset of the Nez Perce War.

**Ellis**   Nez Perce chief. Educated at the Red River Mission School and the grandson of *Hohots Ilppilp*. Appointed as chief of all the Nez Perce by Elijah White.

**Estoweaz**   Nez Perce subchief. Sent to Canada as part of a delegation to encourage the surrender of White Bird.

**Findley, A. B.**   Rancher. His participation in the murder of Blowing Wind would start the Nez Perce War.

**Forse, Albert**   Lieutenant, U.S. Army. Stationed at Fort Walla Walla. Negotiated a reduction in hostilities between Joseph and the white settlers following the death of Blowing Wind during the summer of 1876.

**Frost, Joseph H.**   Established the Clatsop Mission in 1840.

**Gibbon, John**   Colonel, U.S. Army. Responsible for the attack on the Nez Perce at the Battle of the Big Hole.

**Gilliam, Cornelius**   Commanded the Oregon Rifles during the Cayuse War.

**Grant, Ulysses S.**   President of the United States (1869–1877) and architect of the Peace Policy.

**Gray, William**   Methodist missionary under Henry Spalding.

**Grey Eagle**   Cayuse War chief.

**Grover, LaFayette F.**   Governor of the state of Oregon (1870–1877).

**Hahtalekin**   Palouse chief. Killed at the Battle of Big Hole.

**Hale, Calvin**   Oregon Superintendent of Indian Affairs during the signing of the Thief Treaty.

**Haworth, J. M.**   Indian agent at the Quapaw Agency.

**Hayes, Rutherford**   President of the United States (1877–1881).

**Hayt, Ezra**   Commissioner of Indian Affairs (1877–1880).

**Heyoom Moxmox**   (Yellow Grizzly Bear) His criticism promoted *Wahkitits* to attack white settlers.

**Heyoon yoyikt**   Joseph's wife.

**Hill, Tom**   Half Nez Perce, half Delaware warrior who escaped to Canada during the Nez Perce War.

*Hin-mah-tute-ke-kaikt*  (Thunder Eyes), or James. Nez Perce chief on whose land Henry and Eliza Spalding established the Lapwai Mission.

*Hi-yuts-to-henin*  (Rabbit Skin Leggings) Part of the 1831 delegation to St. Louis to request missionaries.

*Hohots-Ilppilp*  (Red Grizzly Bear) Nez Perce chief who met Lewis and Clark in 1805.

*Hophoponmi*  (Noise of Running Feet) Joseph's daughter.

**Howard, Oliver Otis**  General, U.S. Army. Appointed commander of the Columbia in 1874 and responsible for the campaign against the Nez Perce in the summer of 1877.

*Husishusis Kute*  (Bald Head) Palouse chief who participated in the Nez Perce War and was forced into exile with the Nez Perce.

**Ilges, Guido**  Major, U.S. Army. Participated in the Nez Perce War.

*Isaiachalkis*  Cayuse warrior tried and executed for role in the Whitman Massacre.

**Jerome, David**  Peace commissioner during the summer of 1876.

**Jerome, Lovell**  Lieutenant, U.S. Army. Walked into the Nez Perce camp during the Battle of Bear Paw Mountain and was held by the Indians until Joseph was returned.

*Jokais*  (Captain John) Christianized Nez Perce leader.

*Ka-ou-pu*  (Man of the Morning) Part of the 1831 delegation to St. Louis to request missionaries.

*Khap-kha-pon-imi*  (Loose Bark on Trees), or Asenath. Joseph's mother.

*Kimasumpkin*  Cayuse warrior. Tried and executed for role in the Whitman Massacre.

*Kintpuash*  (Captain Jack) Modoc war leader. Led the Modoc War in 1872–1873.

*Klokamas*  Cayuse warrior. Tried and executed for role in the Whitman Massacre.

*Lahmotta*  White Bird Canyon.

**Lawyer**  (*Hallalhotsoot*) Christianized Nez Perce chief who signed the 1863 treaty, known as the Thief Treaty.

**Lee, Daniel**  Methodist missionary to the Nez Perce and nephew of Jason Lee.

**Lee, Henry A. G.**  Led a peace commission during the Cayuse War (1847–1855).

**Lee, Jason**  Reverend. Methodist missionary to the Nez Perce.

**Lewis, Joe**  Half white and half Nez Perce missionary from the East who spread rumors that the Whitmans were poisoning the Indians in order to seize their land. His activities prompted the massacre in 1847.

**Luke**  Christianized Nez Perce Indian who protected Henry Spalding after the Whitman Massacre.

**McConville, Edward**  Led a group of volunteers during the Nez Perce War.

**McLaughlin, James**  Special agent for the Commissioner of Indian Affairs; in 1890 evaluated whether Joseph and his people should be allowed to return home. Denied their request.

**McNall, Wells**  Murdered Nez Perce warrior Blowing Wind in the summer of 1876. His actions would be one of the catalysts that would start the Nez Perce War.

**Meacham, A. B.**  Commissioner of Indian Affairs in Oregon (1869–1872).

**Meek, Joseph**  U.S. marshal during the Cayuse War.

**Miles, Nelson**  General, U.S. Army. Captured the Nez Perce at Bear Paw and used his influence to return them to their homeland after their captivity.

**Monteith, John**  Indian agent on the Lapwai Reservation during the Nez Perce War.

*Neesh-ne-park-ke-ook*  (Cutnose) Chief who met Lewis and Clark in 1805.

**Newell, Robert**  Led a peace commission during the Cayuse War (1847–1855).

**No Heart**  Nez Perce warrior who delayed Howard's advance at the Clearwater River. Killed at the Battle of Big Hole.

**Odneal, T. B.**  Superintendent of Indian Affairs in Oregon (1872–1873).

*Ollokot*  (Frog) Brother of Chief Joseph and war leader of the band. Killed at the Battle of Bear Paw Mountain.

**Ott, Larry**   Settler in the Wallowa Valley who in 1875 killed *Tipyahkanah Siskan* (Eagle Robe).

**Page, Tom**   Settler who signed on with Howard's army to track the Nez Perce.

*Pahkatos Owyeen*   (Five Wounds) Nez Perce War chief. Killed at the Battle of Big Hole.

*Pahkatos Qoh Qoh*   (Five Crows), or Hezekiah. Cayuse chief and Old Joseph's half brother.

**Palmer, Joel**   Led a peace commission during the Cayuse War (1847–1855).

**Perry, David**   Commanded the troops that fought against the Nez Perce at White Bird Canyon.

**Pierce, Franklin**   President of the United States (1853–1857).

**Poker Joe**   Half white and half Nez Perce warrior who joined the fleeing Indians in Montana and assumed control of the band after their defeat at Big Hole.

**Polk, James**   President of the United States (1845–1849).

*Qi'wn*   Sweat Lodge Man.

**Rains, Sevier**   Lieutenant, U.S. Army. Fought in the Nez Perce War.

**Randall, D. B.**   Commanded a company of volunteers during the Nez Perce War; killed following the Battle at the Cottonwood.

**Rawn, Charles**   Captain, U.S. Army. Commanded a small contingent of soldiers and volunteers in Montana. Agreed to allow the Nez Perce to pass his position unmolested.

**Red Wolf**   Christianized Nez Perce chief.

**Reuben**   Christianized Nez Perce chief. Brother-in-law of Chief Joseph.

**Reuben, James**   Christianized nephew of Chief Joseph.

*Sapachesap*   A cave on the Cottonwood Creek where the Nez Perce met at the outset of the Nez Perce War.

*Sarpsis Ilppilp*   (Red Moccasin Tops) Friend of *Wahkitits*. Nez Perce warrior who in avenging his father's death began the Nez Perce War in 1877.

**Schurz, Carl**   Secretary of the Interior (1877–1881).

*Seeyokoon Ilppilp* (Red Spy) Nez Perce warrior.

**Shepard, Cyrus** Methodist missionary to the Nez Perce under Jason Lee.

**Sherman, William Tecumseh** Civil War general and commander of the army during the Nez Perce War.

**Sitting Bull** Sioux war chief who led the attack against Custer in 1876.

**Smith, Asa B.** Established the Kamiah Mission 1839.

**Smith, Edward P.** Commissioner of Indian Affairs (1873–1875).

**Smith, J. Q.** Commissioner of Indian Affairs (1875–1877).

*Sou-Sou-Quee* Cousin of Chief Joseph, often mistaken for an older brother.

**Spalding, Eliza** Established the Lapwai Mission with her husband, Henry, in 1836.

**Spalding, Henry** Established the Lapwai Mission with his wife, Eliza, in 1836.

**Stevens, Isaac** Superintendent of Indian Affairs and governor of Washington State (1853–1857).

**Stickney, William** Peace commissioner during the summer of 1876.

**Sturgis, Samuel** Colonel, U.S. Army. Fought during the Nez Perce War.

**Sutherland, Thomas** War correspondent who reported on the Nez Perce War.

*Takseen* (The Willows) Place where the Nez Perce retreated after the Battle of Big Hole.

*Tamootsin* (Timothy) Contemporary of Old Joseph and early convert to Christianity at the Lapwai Mission and supporter of Henry Spalding.

*Tawis Gee-jumnin* (No Horns on His Head) Part of the 1831 delegation to St. Louis to request missionaries.

*Teto-har-sky* Chief who met Lewis and Clark in 1805.

**Thompson, David** Established a fur-trade post for the North West Company of Montreal in Nez Perce country in 1807.

*Tilokaikt* Cayuse chief who participated in the Whitman Massacre.

*Tipyahkanah Siskan* (Eagle Robe) Nez Perce chief. Father of *Wahkitits*. When Wahkitits avenged his death at the hands of white men, his actions would start the Nez Perce War.

*Tip-yah-lanah* Part of the 1831 delegation to St. Louis to request missionaries.

*Titwatitnáawit* Nez Perce traditional stories.

*Toma Alwawonmi* (Springtime) Joseph's second wife.

*Tomahas* Cayuse warrior who killed Marcus Whitman and began the Whitman Massacre in 1847.

*Tonwitakis* Nez Perce warrior who was called by Henry Spalding to whip Blue Cloak but refused.

*Toohoolhoolzote* Nez Perce chief who favored war during the summer of 1877.

*Tuekakas* (Old Joseph) Nez Perce chief of the Wellamotkin band of Nez Perce and the father of Chief Joseph.

*Tunn-ache-moot-oolt* (Broken Arm) Chief who met Lewis and Clark in 1805.

*Umtippe* (Split Lip) Cayuse chief on whose land the Whitmans established their mission in 1836.

*Wahchumyus* (Rainbow) Nez Perce War chief. Killed at the Battle of Big Hole.

*Wahkitits* (Shore Crossing) Nez Perce warrior whose murder of whites in the Wallowa Valley sparked the Nez Perce War. Killed at the Battle of Big Hole.

*Wala-mot-tinin* (Twisted Hair) Chief who first met Lewis and Clark and the father of Lawyer.

**Walker, Courtney** Methodist missionary to the Nez Perce under Jason Lee.

**Walker, Philip** Methodist missionary to the Nez Perce under Jason Lee.

**Walker, William** Wyandot chief who assisted the Nez Perce in obtaining missionaries in 1832.

*Wa-win-te-pi-ksat* Wife of Chief Joseph.

**Wayakin**   A spirit guide.

**Wetatonmi**   Wife of Ollokot.

**Wettiwetti Howlis**   (Vicious Weasel) Attempted a truce at White Bird Canyon but was fired upon by Arthur Chapman.

**Wetyetmas Wyakaikt**   (Swan Necklace) Friend of *Wahkitits*.

**Whipple, Stephen**   Captain, U.S. Army. Sent to arrest Looking Glass during the outset of the Nez Perce War.

**Whisk-tasket**   Nez Perce chief. Father-in-law of Joseph.

**White Bird**   (*Peo-peo Kis-kiok Hi-hih*) Nez Perce chief who initially favored war during the conflict with the U.S. Army in 1877.

**White, Elijah**   Methodist missionary—often quarreled with Henry Spalding. Later appointed superintendent of Indian Affairs.

**Whitman, Marcus**   Established the Waiilatpu Mission with his wife, Narcissa, in 1836. Killed by Cayuse Indians in 1847.

**Whitman, Narcissa**   Established the Waiilatpu Mission with her husband, Marcus, in 1836. Killed by Cayuse Indians in 1847.

**Wilhautyah**   (Blowing Wind) His murder by Wells McNall in 1876 would serve as the catalyst for the Nez Perce War.

**Wood, Henry Clay**   Aide to General Oliver Otis Howard when he commanded the Department of the Columbia.

**Wottolen**   Nez Perce warrior who had a premonition of defeat before the Battle at Bear Paw.

**Wyeth, Nathaniel**   Trapper with the American Fur Company.

**Yom-park-kar-tim**   (Five Big Hearts) Chief who met Lewis and Clark in 1805.

**Young Chief**   Cayuse chief and ally of Chief Joseph.

# BIBLIOGRAPHY

Brown, Mark Herbert. *The Flight of the Nez Perce*. Lincoln, NE: Bison Books, 1982.

Carlson, Paul. *The Plains Indians*. College Station: Texas A & M University Press, 1998.

Chief Joseph. *That All People May Be One People, Send Rain to Wash the Face of the Earth*. Kooskia, ID: Mountain Meadow Press, 1995.

Clark, William, and Meriwether Lewis. *Journals of the Lewis and Clark Expedition*. Edited by Gary E. Moulton. Lincoln: University of Nebraska, 2003.

Etulain, Richard W., and Glenda Riley. *Chiefs and Generals: Nine Men Who Shaped the American West*. Golden, CO: Fulcrum Publishing, 2004.

Gay, E. Jane. *With the Nez Perces: Alice Fletcher in the Field 1889–1892*. Edited by Frederick E. Hoxie and Joan T. Mark. Lincoln: University of Nebraska Press, 1981.

Greene, Jerome, and Alvin Josephy, Jr., *Nez Perce Summer, 1877: The U.S. Army and the Nee-Me-Poo Crisis*. Helena, MT: Montana Historical Society, 2001.

Hampton, Bruce. *Children of Grace: The Nez Perce War of 1877*. New York: H. Holt Publishers, 1994.

Howard, Oliver Otis. *Autobiography of Oliver Otis Howard, Major-General, United States Army*. New York: Baker & Taylor, 1908.

Howard, Oliver Otis. *Nez Perce Joseph: An Account of His Ancestors, His Lands, His Confederates, His Enemies, His Murders.* Charleston, SC: Bibliolife, 2009.

Josephy, Alvin M. *The Nez Perce Indians and the Opening of the Northwest.* New York: Houghton Mifflin, 1997.

Laughy, Linwood. *In Pursuit of the Nez Perces: The Nez Perce War of 1877.* Wrangell, AK: Mountain Meadow Press, 1993.

Lavender, David. *Let Me Be Free: The Nez Perce Tragedy.* Norman: University of Oklahoma Press, 1982.

Lewis, Meriwether, and William Clark. *The Journals of the Lewis and Clark Expedition.* Edited by Gary E Moulton. Lincoln: University of Nebraska Press, 2003.

Libby, Orin Grant, II, ed. *Collection of the State Historical Society of North Dakota.* Bismarck, ND: Tribune State Printers and Binders, 1908.

Marshall, S.L.A. *Crimsoned Prairies: The Indian Wars.* New York: Da Capo Press, 1972.

McCoy, Robert R. *Chief Joseph, Yellow Wolf, and the Creation of Nez Perce History in the Pacific Northwest.* New York: Routledge, 2004.

McWhorter, L. V. *Yellow Wolf: His Own Story.* Caldwell, ID: Caxton Press, 2008.

Mooney, James. *The Ghost-Dance Religion and the Sioux Outbreak of 1890.* Lincoln: University of Nebraska Press, 1991.

Moulton, Candy. *Chief Joseph: Guardian of the People.* New York: Macmillan, 2006.

Murray, Keith A. *The Modocs and Their War.* Norman: University of Oklahoma Press, 1959.

Nerburn, Kent. *Chief Joseph and the Flight of the Nez Perce: The Untold Story of an American Tragedy.* San Francisco: Harper Collins Publishers, 2005.

Schofield, Brian. *Selling Your Father's Bones: America's 140 Year War Against the Nez Perce Tribe.* New York: Simon & Schuster, 2009.

Spinden, Herbert Joseph. *The Nez Perce Indians.* White Fish, MT: Kessinger Publishers, 2007.

U.S. War Department. *Annual Report of the Secretary of War, Volume 1.* Washington: U.S. Government Printing Office, 1877.

## JOURNAL ARTICLES

Aoki, Harou. "Nez Perce and Proto-Sahaptian Kinship Terms." *International Journal of American Linguistics* 32, no. 4 (October 1966): 357–68.

Haines, Francis. "The Nez Perce Delegation to St. Louis in 1831." *The Pacific Historical Review* 6, no. 1 (March 1937): 71–78.

Jessett, Thomas. "The Church of England in the Old Oregon Country." *Church History* 22, no. 3 (September 1953): 219–26.

Packard, R. L. "Notes on the Mythology and Religion of the Nez Perces." *The Journal of American Folklore* 4, no. 15 (October–December 1891): 327–30.

Rude, Noel. "Topicality, Transivity, and the Direct Object in Nez Perce." *International Journal of American Linguistics* 52, no. 2 (April 1986): 124–53.

Speck, Frank G. "The Family Hunting Band as the Basis of Algonkian Social Organization." *American Anthropologist* 9, no. 2 (April–June 1915): 289–305.

Trafzer, Clifford E., and Margery A. Beach. "Smohalla, the Washani, and Religion as a Factor in Northwestern Indian History." *American Indian Quarterly* 9, no. 3 (Summer 1985): 309–24.

Walker, Deward E. "The Nez Perce Sweatbath Complex: An Acculturational Analysis." *Southwestern Journal of Anthropology* 22, no. 2 (Summer 1966): 133–71.

# WEB SOURCES

National Geographic. "Lewis and Clark." *Lewis and Clark*. Available from http://www.nationalgeographic.com/lewisandclark (accessed May 4, 2009).

National Park Service. "Lewis and Clark National Historic Trail." *Journey of Discovery*. Available from http://www.nps.gov (accessed March 3, 2009).

Nez Perce Tribe. "Nez Perce Tribe History." *Nez Perce Tribe Website*. Available from http://www.nezperce.org (accessed March 8, 2009).

# INDEX

## About the Author

VANESSA GUNTHER is an adjunct professor of history at the California State University in Fullerton, California. She completed her Ph.D. in Native American history at the University of California in Riverside in 2001. Gunther has contributed several encyclopedic entries and essays to compilations about the law and Native Americans in the 19th and 20th centuries and is the author of *Ambiguous Justice*. She currently lives in Fullerton, California.